D0290497

⁶/₉₉ CL

WEST
‹INDIES›

MAJOR WORLD NATIONS

WEST INDIES

Suzanne Anthony

CHELSEA HOUSE PUBLISHERS
Philadelphia

Chelsea House Publishers

Contributing Author: Derek Davis

First Printing

1 3 5 7 9 8 6 4 2

Library of Congress Cataloging-in-Publication Data

Anthony, Suzanne.
West Indies.

(Major World Nations)
Includes index.
Summary: An overview of the history, geography, economy,
government, people, and culture of the West Indies.
1. West Indies—Juvenile literature.   [1. West Indies]
I. Title.   II. Series.
F1608.3.A57   1989   972.9   88-30434
ISBN 0-7910-4772-5

‹CONTENTS›

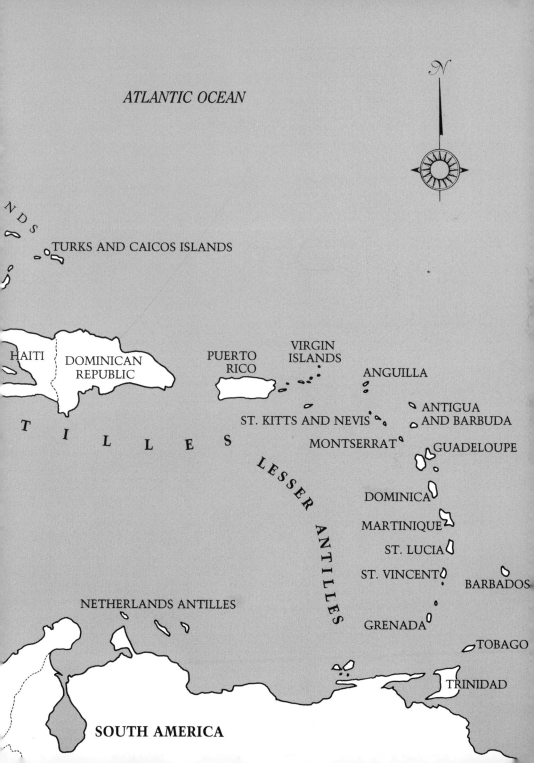

◄ FACTS AT A GLANCE ►

West Indies

Area	91,000 square miles (236,600 sq km)
Population	36 million
Ethnic Groups	White, black, black/white mix, Caribbean Indian, East Indian
Economic Base	Agriculture (sugarcane, bananas, coffee), tourism, financial services, petroleum

Cuba

Area	44,218 square miles (114,524 sq km)
Population	11 million
Population Density	250 people per square mile (95 per sq km)
Capital	Havana
Language	Spanish
Ethnic Groups	White, Black/white mix, Chinese, Japanese
Form of Government	Communist state, headed by the leader of Communist party
Economic Base	Agriculture (sugarcane, tobacco), petroleum
Gross Domestic Product (GDP) per person	$1,300

Dominican Republic

Area	18,704 square miles (48,630 sq km)
Population	8 million
Population Density	425 people per square mile (165 per sq km)
Capital	Santo Domingo
Language	Spanish
Ethnic Groups	White/black mix, white, black, Japanese
Form of Government	Republic with elected president
Economic Base	Agriculture (sugarcane, coffee), tourism
GDP per person	$3,400

Haiti

Area	10,714 square miles (27,856 sq km)
Population	7 million
Population Density	650 people per square mile (240 per sq km)
Capital	Port-au-Prince
Language	French, Creole (French/African mix)
Ethnic Groups	Black, black/white mix
Form of Government	Republic with elected president
Economic Base	Agriculture (coffee, sugarcane, bananas), electronics
GDP per person	$1,000

Jamaica

Area	4,411 square miles (11,424 sq km)
Population	2.6 million
Population Density	590 people per square mile (225 per sq km)

Capital	Kingston
Language	English
Ethnic Groups	Black, black/white mix, white
Form of Government	Parliamentary state within Commonwealth of Nations
Economic Base	Bauxite, agriculture (sugarcane, bananas), tourism
GDP per person	$3,200

Puerto Rico

Area	3,435 square miles (8,931 sq km)
Population	3.8 million
Population Density	1,100 people per square mile (425 per sq km)
Capital	San Juan
Languages	Spanish, English
Ethnic Groups	Black/white mix, white, black
Form of Government	Commonwealth associated with the United States, with elected governor
Economic Base	Industry (pharmaceuticals, textiles), agriculture (sugarcane, coffee), tourism
GDP per person	$7,800

Anguilla

Area	35 square miles (91 sq km)
Population	10,400
Population Density	295 people per square mile (115 per sq km)
Capital	The Valley
Language	English
Ethnic Groups	Black, white

Form of Government	Dependent territory of the United Kingdom
Economic Base	Tourism, financial services, fishing
GDP per person	$7,600

Antigua and Barbuda

Area	171 square miles (445 sq km)
Population	66,000
Population Density	385 people per square mile (150 per sq km)
Capital	St. John's
Language	English
Ethnic Groups	Black, white
Form of Government	Parliamentary state within Commonwealth of Nations
Economic Base	Agriculture (sugarcane, cotton), tourism
GDP per person	$6,600

Barbados

Area	166 square miles (432 sq km)
Population	260,000
Population Density	1,565 people per square mile (605 per sq km)
Capital	Bridgetown
Language	English
Ethnic Groups	Black, white
Form of Government	Parliamentary state within Commonwealth of Nations
Economic Base	Petroleum and natural gas, sugarcane, tourism
GDP per person	$9,800

Dominica

Area	290 square miles (754 sq km)
Population	83,000
Population Density	285 people per square mile (110 per sq km)
Capital	Roseau
Language	English
Ethnic Groups	Black, black/white mix, white, Syrian, Caribbean Indian
Form of Government	Parliamentary state within Commonwealth of Nations
Economic Base	Agriculture (bananas, citrus fruits), pumice, tourism
GDP per person	$2,450

Grenada

Area	133 square miles (344 sq km)
Population	95,000
Population Density	715 people per square mile (275 per sq km)
Capital	St. George's
Language	English
Ethnic Groups	Black, black/white mix, East Indian, white
Form of Government	Parliamentary state within Commonwealth of Nations
Economic Base	Agriculture (spices, bananas), tourism
GDP per person	$3,000

Guadeloupe

Area	687 square miles (1,786 sq km)
Population	410,000

Population Density	600 people per square mile (230 per sq km)
Capital	Basse-Terre
Language	French, Creole
Ethnic Groups	Black, black/white mix, white
Form of Government	Overseas department of France
Economic Base	Tourism, agriculture (bananas, sugarcane)
GDP per person	$9,200

Martinique

Area	431 square miles (1,121 sq km)
Population	400,000
Population Density	930 people per square mile (360 per sq km)
Capital	Fort-de-France
Language	French
Ethnic Groups	Black, white
Form of Government	Overseas department of France
Economic Base	Agriculture (sugarcane, bananas), tourism
GDP per person	$10,000

Montserrat

Area	39 square miles (101 sq km)
Population	12,700
Population Density	325 people per square mile (125 per sq km)
Capital	Plymouth
Language	English

Ethnic Groups	White, black, black/white mix
Form of Government	Dependent territory of the United Kingdom
Economic Base	Tourism, electronics
GDP per person	$4,500

Netherlands Antilles

Area	309 square miles (800 sq km)
Population	210,000
Population Density	685 people per square mile (265 per sq km)
Capital	Willemstad
Language	Dutch
Ethnic Groups	White, black, black/white mix, Caribbean Indian, Chinese, East Indian
Form of Government	Part of Kingdom of the Netherlands
Economic Base	Petroleum, tourism, financial services
GDP per person	$10,400

Aruba

Area	75 square miles (194 sq km)
Population	65,000
Population Density	865 people per square mile (335 per sq km)
Capital	Oranjestad
Language	Dutch
Ethnic Groups	White, Caribbean Indian/white mix, Caribbean Indian
Form of Government	Part of Kingdom of the Netherlands

Economic Base	Tourism, financial services, petroleum
GDP per person	$18,000

St. Kitts and Nevis

Area	101 square miles (263 sq km)
Population	41,000
Population Density	405 people per square mile (155 per sq km)
Capital	Basseterre
Language	English
Ethnic Groups	Black, black/white mix
Form of Government	Parliamentary state within Commonwealth of Nations (Nevis is expected to become independent of St. Kitts)
Economic Base	Agriculture (sugarcane, cotton), tourism
GDP per person	$5,380

St. Lucia

Area	238 square miles (616 sq km)
Population	160,000
Population Density	670 people per square mile (260 per sq km)
Capital	Castries
Language	English
Ethnic Groups	Black, black/white mix, white, East Indian
Form of Government	Parliamentary state within Commonwealth of Nations
Economic Base	Agriculture (bananas), tourism
GDP per person	$4,080

St. Vincent and the Grenadines

Area	150 square miles (390 sq km)
Population	120,000
Population Density	800 people per square mile (305 per sq km)
Capital	Kingstown
Language	English
Ethnic Groups	Black, black/white mix, white, East Indian
Form of Government	Parliamentary state within Commonwealth of Nations
Economic Base	Agriculture (bananas), tourism
GDP per person	$2,060

Trinidad and Tobago

Area	1,980 square miles (5,148 sq km)
Population	1.3 million
Population Density	655 people per square mile (250 per sq km)
Capital	Port-of-Spain
Language	English
Ethnic Groups	Black, East Indian, black/white mix, white
Form of Government	Parliamentary state within Commonwealth of Nations
Economic Base	Petroleum, tourism, agriculture (sugarcane, cocoa)
GDP per person	$12,100

British Virgin Islands

Area	59 square miles (153 sq km)
Population	13,000
Population Density	220 people per square mile (85 per sq km)

Capital	Road Town
Language	English
Ethnic Groups	Black, black/white mix, white
Form of Government	Dependent territory of the United Kingdom
Economic Base	Tourism, financial services, agriculture (livestock)
GDP per person	$10,600

U.S. Virgin Islands

Area	133 square miles (344 sq km)
Population	100,000
Population Density	750 people per square mile (290 per sq km)
Capital	Charlotte Amalie
Language	English
Ethnic Groups	Black, black/white mix, white, Chacha (French descent)
Form of Government	Unincorporated territory of the United States with elected governor
Economic Base	Tourism, petroleum, electronics
GDP per person	$12,500

The Bahamas

Area	5,382 square miles (13,939 sq km)
Population	270,000
Population Density	50 people per square mile (20 per sq km)
Capital	Nassau
Language	English

Ethnic Groups	Black, black/white mix, white
Form of Government	Parliamentary state within Commonwealth of Nations
Economic Base	Tourism, financial services, petroleum
GDP per person	$18,700

Bermuda

Area	20 square miles (52 sq km)
Population	62,000
Population Density	3,100 people per square mile (1,190 per sq km)
Capital	Hamilton
Language	English
Ethnic Groups	Black, white
Form of Government	Dependent territory of the United Kingdom
Economic Base	Tourism, financial services
GDP per person	$28,000

Cayman Islands

Area	102 square miles (265 sq km)
Population	35,000
Population Density	350 people per square mile (135 per sq km)
Capital	George Town
Language	English
Ethnic Groups	White, black
Form of Government	Dependent territory of the United Kingdom
Economic Base	Tourism, financial services
GDP per person	$22,500

Turks and Caicos Islands

Area	193 square miles (502 sq km)
Population	14,000
Population Density	73 people per square mile (28 per sq km)
Capital	Grand Turk
Language	English
Ethnic Groups	Black, black/white mix, white
Form of Government	Dependent territory of the United Kingdom
Economic Base	Tourism, fishing, financial services
GDP per person	$6,000

◄HISTORY AT A GLANCE►

Cuba

1492   Christopher Columbus discovers Cuba and claims it for Spain during his first voyage to the New World.

1511   Diego Velázquez, a Spaniard, founds Baracoa, Cuba's first permanent settlement.

1500s   Cuba serves as a starting point for Spanish exploration of Florida, the Yucátan, and the Gulf of Mexico's coast.

1600s   The colony survives a series of hurricanes, epidemics, pirate attacks, and territorial battles.

1700s   Sugarcane cultivation becomes the major economic activity; African slaves are imported to work in the fields.

1838 to 1880   Cuba's sugar industry becomes the most mechanized and productive in the world.

1895   Cuban rebels begin fighting for Cuba's independence from Spain.

1898   The United States joins in the war against Spain.

1899   Cuban independence begins. United States troops occupy the new nation.

1902   A new republican constitution takes effect. U.S. troops withdraw.

1958   Fidel Castro overthrows President Fulgencio Batista. With Castro as president and prime minister, the Communist party of Cuba takes control of the government.

1960   Cuba establishes diplomatic and trade relations with the Soviet Union.

1961   With support from the United States, a band of Cuban exiles lands at the Bay of Pigs in an unsuccessful attempt to overthrow Castro's government.

1976   The first elections under a new socialist constitution allow Cubans to elect representatives to municipal assemblies.

1989 to 1993   Withdrawal of Soviet aid and increased American sanctions lead to economic disaster.

Dominican Republic

1492   Columbus lands on the island of Hispaniola during his first voyage to the New World. He establishes a colony that is later moved to the site of present-day Santo Domingo.

1550 to 1795   Spain loses interest in its colony on Hispaniola. Soldiers and pirates from many nations invade the island. The economy suffers, and many Spanish settlers leave for more prosperous colonies. French slave-owners develop a sugarcane industry on the western third of the island, in the area that later becomes Haiti.

1795   Defeated in European wars, Spain gives up the island to France. Haiti's slaves revolt, throwing off French rule and taking over the eastern two-thirds of the island. The British fleet helps the Hispaniolans drive the Haitians back.

1809   The colony of Hispaniola—now the eastern two-thirds of the island—is reunited with Spain. It is called Santo Domingo.

1821	Santo Domingo declares its independence as the Dominican Republic.
1822 to 1844	The Dominican Republic is occupied by Haitian forces.
1844 to 1930	The Haitians are driven out after a long struggle. Under a series of short-lived, unstable governments, the Dominican Republic achieves some modernization but remains poor and politically repressive. Spain and the United States each take control of the government for brief periods.
1930	Rafael Trujillo seizes power and rules as a strict dictator for 31 years. The economy improves but civil rights are almost abolished.
1961	Trujillo is assassinated by members of his own army. A conservative government takes power.
1965	A revolution against the conservative government is defeated by United States forces.
1978	The Dominican Republic celebrates the first transfer in its history from one democratically elected president to another and begins a period of economic and social reforms.

Haiti

1492	Columbus lands on the island of Hispaniola during his first voyage to the New World. The island becomes a Spanish colony.
1600s	French pirates establish plantations on the western end of the island.
1697	Spain formally gives the western third of Hispaniola to France. The French name their new colony Saint Domingue.

1700s	Sugar, coffee, cocoa, cotton, and indigo make Saint Domingue the most prosperous colony in the Americas.
1790s	Led by Toussaint Louverture, the slaves of Saint Domingue rise in revolt.
1804	The blacks of Saint Domingue declare the island of Hispaniola independent under the Arawak Indian name Haiti.
1822	Haiti invades Santo Domingo and controls it until 1844.
1843 to 1915	Haiti has 20 rulers. Most are assassinated or overthrown.
1915 to 1934	To protect American military and economic interests, U.S. Marines occupy Haiti.
1946 to 1956	Military juntas rule the country.
1957	François Duvalier, called Papa Doc, is elected president. With the aid of terrorism, he holds power until his death in 1971.
1971	Jean-Claude Duvalier, called Baby Doc, succeeds his father as president.
1986 to 1990	After Baby Doc is driven from office, military governments rule the country.
1991	Elected president Jean-Bertrand Aristide is removed in a coup.
1994	Aristide and democratic government are allowed to return under threat of invasion by United Nations forces.

Jamaica

1494	Columbus discovers Jamaica during his second voyage to the New World.

1655   The British capture Jamaica.

mid-1600s   Jamaica becomes the haunt of buccaneers and pirates, who use Port Royal as their base.

1660   The Spaniards are completely driven out of the colony; their black slaves form Maroon societies. Armed by the Spanish, the Maroon people fight the British for many years.

1866   Jamaica becomes a crown colony, with a British-appointed governor at its head.

1958 to 1962   Jamaica is a member of the Federation of the West Indies.

1962   Jamaica becomes an independent dominion within the Commonwealth of Nations.

1980   Edward Seaga is elected prime minister and cuts ties with Cuba. He attempts to strengthen a capitalist democracy based on tourism and new industries.

Puerto Rico

1493   During his second voyage to the New World, Columbus claims the island for Spain.

1508   Juan Ponce de León explores the island. He discovers the harbor at San Juan that gives the island its name (Puerto Rico means "Rich Port").

1800s   Spain allows the colony's residents to elect representatives to the Spanish parliament, but the colony remains under the rule of military governors.

1898   United States forces capture Puerto Rico in the Spanish-American War. The island becomes a U.S. territory.

1947 The U.S. grants Puerto Ricans the right to elect their governor.

currently A movement for complete independence from the U.S. gains strength in Puerto Rico. However, some citizens want the island to become the 51st member of the United States. The majority of Puerto Ricans want to continue the existing relationship.

Anguilla

1493 Columbus discovers the island during his second voyage to the New World.

1650 Anguilla becomes a British colony.

1882 Anguilla, St. Christopher, and Nevis unite in a federation.

1967 The federation becomes an independent state associated with the United Kingdom. The same year, Anguilla withdraws from the federation.

1971 Anguilla comes under direct British control.

Antigua and Barbuda

1493 Columbus visits Antigua.

1628 Barbuda is colonized by the Codrington family of England. It becomes their property in 1680.

1666 The French raid Antigua.

late 1600s Sugarcane replaces tobacco as the chief crop.

late 1800s Barbuda becomes a crown colony associated with Antigua.

1958 to 1962 Antigua is a member of the Federation of the West Indies.

1981 Antigua and Barbuda form an independent state within the Commonwealth of Nations.

Barbados

early 1500s	Spain raids Barbados in search of slaves to work on the plantations of Hispaniola.
1550	After eliminating the native Indian population, Spain lets its claim to the island lapse.
early 1620s	Several English groups land on the island and claim it for England.
1700s	Sugarcane becomes the chief crop and many African slaves are imported to work on the plantations.
1834	Slavery is abolished.
1937	Barbadians riot to protest economic depression and neglect by Great Britain.
1944 to 1954	Barbados gradually becomes self-governing.
1966	Barbados becomes an independent nation within the Commonwealth of Nations.
currently	Barbados is politically and economically stable.

Dominica

1493	Columbus sights the island.
1632	The first colonists arrive on the island from France.
1783	The British capture the island.
1883 to 1940	Dominica is part of the Leeward Islands colony of Great Britain.
1958 to 1962	Dominica is part of the Federation of the West Indies.
1978	Dominica achieves independence.
1980s and 1990s	The country's economy remains marginal, though slowly improving.

Grenada

1498	Columbus discovers the island but sails past it.
1650	French settlers from Martinique establish a small colony.
1700s	The French and British fight to control Grenada.
1783	The British win control of the island under the Treaty of Versailles.
1834	Slavery is abolished.
1885 to 1958	Grenada is the headquarters of the British Windward Islands colony.
1958 to 1962	Grenada is a member of the Federation of the West Indies.
1974	Grenada becomes an independent nation.
1979	Prime Minister Eric Gairy is overthrown in a coup led by Maurice Bishop, who establishes a socialist government.
1983	Bishop's government is overthrown in a coup. United States military forces occupy the island to restore order and prevent the Socialists from regaining power.
1984	The Grenada constitution, suspended in 1979, is reinstated, followed by free elections and a democratic government.

Guadeloupe

1493	Columbus visits the territory's two main islands.
1515 to 1523	The Carib Indians fight off three Spanish attempts at colonization.

1620	The French establish a colony on Guadeloupe.
1674	Guadeloupe becomes the property of the French monarch. It is administered as a dependency of Martinique.
1759 to 1763	The British occupy Guadeloupe.
1775	Guadeloupe becomes a colony of France and is no longer treated as a dependency of Martinique.
1946	Guadeloupe is given the status of a department, or administrative district, of France.
1960s and 1970s	Guadeloupe is given greater control of its internal affairs, but some islanders call for complete independence from France.
1976	The eruption of the volcano Soufrière causes great damage.

Martinique

1493	Columbus sights the island.
1502	During his fourth voyage, Columbus lands on the island.
1635	A French colony is founded and quickly becomes prosperous.
1674	Martinique becomes a property of the French monarch. A plantation economy, based on slave labor imported from Africa, develops.
1789 to 1822	Three slave uprisings occur and are quelled by troops.
1848	The French abolish slavery.
1902	Mont Pelée erupts, killing 30,000 people and destroying the town of Saint Pierre.

1946	Martinique becomes a department, or administrative district, of France.
1958	Martinique votes to become part of French Fifth Republic.
currently	Tourism replaces bananas as focus of economy.

Montserrat

1493	Columbus sights the island.
1632	Irish and English settlers arrive.
1664 to 1783	Montserrat changes hands between the French and British.
1783	The Treaty of Versailles restores the island to England.
1834	Slavery is abolished.
1871 to 1956	The island is part of the British Leeward Islands colony.
1958 to 1962	Montserrat is a member of the Federation of the West Indies.
1978	Elections won by party favoring independence, but the issue is later set aside.
1995 to 1997	Prolonged eruptions of Soufrière Hills volcano lead to evacuation of two-thirds of the island's population and the closing of the capital city, Plymouth.

Netherlands Antilles and Aruba

1490s	Curaçao, Bonaire, Aruba, and Sint Maarten are discovered by Spanish mariners.
1600s	The Dutch take control of the islands and develop a prosperous economy based on slavetrading, smuggling, and farming.

1648	Dutch and French settlers divide the island. The Dutch obtain the smaller but more valuable part, which they call Sint Maarten.
until 1900s	The islands remain Dutch colonies, although the British control them for several brief periods.
1954	The six islands of the Netherlands Antilles form a federation and are made part of the Netherlands.
1986	Aruba separates from the Netherlands Antilles federation and forms an autonomous government under Dutch control.

St. Kitts and Nevis

1493	Columbus sights both islands.
1623	English settlers arrive on St. Christopher and shorten the name to St. Kitts. French settlers soon follow.
1628	The English settle Nevis, which soon becomes prosperous.
until 1800s	St. Kitts changes hands several times between the British and French. Nevis withstands attacks by the Spanish and French.
1882	St. Kitts, Nevis, and Anguilla are united into a federation.
1967	The three-island federation becomes an independent state associated with the United Kingdom. Anguilla withdraws from the federation.
1983	St. Kitts and Nevis becomes an independent nation within the Commonwealth of Nations.
currently	Nevis seeks independence from St. Kitts.

St. Lucia

by 1500	The island is discovered, possibly by Columbus.
1650	The French establish a settlement.
1700s	St. Lucia changes hands between the British and French fourteen times.
1814	The Treaty of Paris awards the island to Britain.
1838 to 1885	St. Lucia is part of the Windward Islands colony, administered from Barbados.
1958 to 1962	St. Lucia is a member of the Federation of the West Indies.
1967	St. Lucia becomes a state associated with the United Kingdom.
1979	St. Lucia becomes an independent parliamentary state within the Commonwealth of Nations.

St. Vincent and the Grenadines

1498	Columbus possibly visits St. Vincent.
1673	African slaves are shipwrecked on St. Vincent; they are the first non-Indian settlers.
1700s	British and the French battle for control of St. Vincent.
1783	Britain wins control of St. Vincent.
1795	Supported by the French in Martinique, the Carib Indians rise in revolt against British rule. The British crush the revolt and expel the Indians.
1800s	Sugarcane becomes the island's main product. Black slaves and, later, East Indian laborers, are brought to St. Vincent to work the plantations.

1958 to 1962	St. Vincent is a member of the Federation of the West Indies.
1969	St. Vincent becomes a state associated with the United Kingdom.
1979	St. Vincent and the Grenadines become an independent nation within the Commonwealth of Nations. An explosion of the volcano Soufrière causes widespread economic damage.

Trinidad and Tobago

1498	During his third voyage to the New World, Columbus reaches Trinidad and sights Tobago.
until 1797	Spain neglects its colony on Trinidad. France, Spain, England, and Holland fight over Tobago.
1797	Spain surrenders Trinidad to Britain.
1802	Britain acquires Tobago.
1889	Britain unites Trinidad and Tobago into one colony.
1962	The colony wins independence. Poverty and unemployment plague the new nation.
1976	Trinidad and Tobago adopts a new constitution.
currently	The government is attempting to reduce the islands' economic dependence on petroleum.

Virgin Islands

1493	Columbus discovers the Virgin Islands.
1555	Spain claims the islands.
1648	Dutch buccaneers settle on Tortola.
1666	English planters take over Tortola. Denmark starts a new colony in St. Thomas.

1672	Tortola becomes part of the British Leeward Islands colony.
1700s	Danes colonize St. Croix, St. John, and the other western islands.
1917	The United States buys the Danish West Indies from Denmark.
1960	The Leeward Islands become a British crown colony.
1967	The British islands are given a ministerial government for internal affairs.
1971	The U.S. Virgin Islands elect their first governor.

The Bahamas

1492	Columbus lands in the Bahamas. He claims them for Spain, but Spain does not colonize.
mid-1600s	British settlers from Bermuda arrive in the Bahamas.
late 1600s	The islands become the haunt of pirates and are raided by the Spanish and French.
1717	The islands come under British control. Woodes Rogers is appointed governor. He ends piracy in the islands.
1729	The islands' first representative assembly meets.
1834	Slavery is abolished.
1973	The Bahamas achieves full independence.

Bermuda

early 1500s	Juan Bermúdez, a Spanish navigator, possibly discovers Bermuda.
1609	Shipwrecked English settlers start a colony.

1612	Bermuda becomes the property of the British Virginia Company.
1684	The islands become the property of the British monarch.
1900s	A tourist industry develops.
currently	Bermuda is prosperous and stable.

Cayman Islands

1503	Columbus sights the islands during his last voyage to the West Indies.
1700s	British settlers from Jamaica arrive. Pirates and outlaws hide in the Caymans.
1877	The three islands are united into a single colony.
1972	A new constitution allows the islanders self-government in most internal affairs.

Turks and Caicos Islands

1512	The Spanish explorer Juan Ponce de León discovers the islands and claims them for Spain.
1678	Settlers from Bermuda establish a salt-panning industry.
early 1800s	The Bahamas colony takes over the islands.
1874 to 1959	The islands are a dependency of Jamaica.
1976	The islands, now under direct British control, receive a new constitution.
1980 to present	Despite elections that produce a majority favoring independence, the nation changes course and decides to remain a dependent territory of the United Kingdom.

Christopher Columbus, who launched an era of New World exploration in 1492, made four voyages to the West Indies—but believed they were Asian islands.

The West Indies and the World

Late at night on October 11, 1492, an event occurred that changed the world forever. Italian navigator Christopher Columbus, sailing under the Spanish flag, sighted a dim light flickering in the darkness. He had been at sea for 33 days, sailing westward from Spain in the hope of discovering a new route to India and the rich Spice Islands of Southeast Asia. That dim light—probably the glow of a fisherman's fire—was Columbus's first glimpse of what he thought were the Spice Islands. In reality, he had found the islands of the West Indies and—invisible to him but stretching far to the north and south—the vast continents of the Americas.

The next day, Columbus landed on a small island that he named San Salvador; most scholars agree that it was the island in the Bahamas that is now called Samana Cay. Because he believed he had arrived in the Spice Islands, or East Indies, he called the native people he found there Indians; thus the native peoples of all the Americas came to be called Indians. After leaving San Salvador, Columbus sailed to other islands, where he found Indians, trees, and fish, but not a trace of the spices, gems, and silks that he sought.

Columbus was not the first European to visit the New World. It is almost certain that roving seamen from Scandinavia and Iceland

Columbus found the islands inhabited by hunting and fishing peoples, whom he called "Indians."

settled in North America centuries before. Their colonies in Greenland and North America died out, however, and the news of their voyages did not travel through the rest of the world. Only after Columbus's return to Spain did Europeans begin to seek adventure and profit westward across the Atlantic Ocean.

After four voyages to the Caribbean Sea, Columbus died in 1506, still believing that he had reached the Far East—and that India and the Spice Islands lay near the islands he had visited. Within a few years of his death, however, other explorers proved Columbus wrong. Columbus had found not a new sea route but a whole New World. Explorers realized that the world included more than the ancient continents of Europe, Africa, and Asia. The great age of exploration began.

The many islands Columbus visited were called the West Indies. Other West Indian islands were soon charted, along with Florida, Mexico, Central America, and the Guyana coast of South America. Early in the 16th century, Spain and the other nations of Europe set out to explore and colonize the Americas. The West Indies received the first colonists in the New World and became the first page in a new chapter of world history.

But the West Indies never became rich and powerful countries. Today, political instability, racial conflict, economic depression, and high unemployment trouble some of the islands. Most of the islands are quite poor, with few or no natural resources. Sugarcane cultivation and tourism are their major sources of income, although several of the islands have profitable oil refineries. Most of the island governments in the region depend on large amounts of foreign aid.

Each of the thousands of large and small islands in the West Indies was at one time the colony of a powerful European nation: Spain, France, Britain, Holland, Denmark, or Sweden. Some islands changed hands dozens of times as the European powers fought for supremacy in the Caribbean and elsewhere. Today, the region is a mixture of independent nations (some including more than one island) and territories still administered by the former colonial powers. The territories and many of the independent states have close ties with their former rulers and rely on them for financial aid.

Many different types of government appear in the West Indies, from the Communist regime of Fidel Castro in Cuba to the parliamentary democracy of Barbados and the colonial status of the Virgin Islands. Of all the West Indian nations, only Cuba has played a significant role in international affairs, lending its support to Communist movements in Africa and Central America during the 1960s and 1970s. Most West Indian nations and territories direct their energies inward, concentrating on establishing or maintaining orderly governments and improving their economies.

Although agriculture and new industries are important economic activities, West Indian economies will most likely improve through the growth of tourism. Ever since the tourist industry got its start in Bermuda early in the 20th century, the West Indies have been the playground of vacationers from North and South America and Europe. The islands hope to attract still more tourists. Hotels, roads, and airports are under construction throughout the West Indies. The islands offer powerful attractions: balmy tropical weather, swaying palm trees and brilliant exotic flowers, sandy beaches, warm waters, and a unique and colorful culture.

This culture is the most distinctive feature of the West Indies. The region is a true melting pot—a place where people from many different cultures have merged to create something totally new. The

The vegetables and fruits of the Bahamas are quite typical of the islands' agricultural richness.

population of the islands has many roots: native Arawak and Carib Indians; Europeans from Spain, Britain, France, and other nations; West Africans brought to the islands as slaves; and Asians who came to work the sugarcane plantations and stayed to raise families.

These people of different races and cultures often intermarried. As a result, a large percentage of the West Indian population is of mixed race (called *mestizo* on Spanish-speaking islands). Through intermarriage and generations of living side by side, the different ethnic groups have contributed to the unique West Indian culture called Creole (from the Spanish word *criollo*, meaning "locally raised").

Creole culture has its own languages, religions, foods, festivals, and art forms. British sports, African gods, Malaysian spices, Dutch windmills, Indonesian and North African food crops, Spanish saints, and hundreds of other cultural elements are mingled together in the Caribbean today. Each of the many nations in the West Indies has made a unique contribution to Creole culture.

Although the West Indies form a diverse region, not a single nation, each island shares the natural beauty and distinctive culture of the Caribbean. These two elements—tropical beauty and Creole culture—are the West Indies' gifts to the world.

Water shortage is a constant problem on many West Indian islands. In Jamaica, farmers use irrigation canals and simple dams to bring water from the lush eastern mountains to their fields during the dry season.

Geography and History

Most of the islands in the West Indies are part of an island group called the Antilles (pronounced an-TILL-eze). The Antilles form an archipelago (island chain) that runs in a 1,500-mile (2,400-kilometer) arc between North and South America. The Antilles archipelago separates the Atlantic Ocean to the east from the deep basin of the Caribbean Sea to the west.

The Antilles are traditionally divided into two groups, the Greater and the Lesser Antilles. The Greater Antilles include the larger islands in the western part of the archipelago: Cuba, Hispaniola (the island divided between the nations of Haiti and the Dominican Republic), Jamaica, and Puerto Rico. The Lesser Antilles include the smaller islands, from the Virgin Islands south to Trinidad and Tobago.

With a few exceptions, the islands of the Antilles are really the tops of a range of mountains called the Caribbean Andes. These mountains sank beneath the sea millions of years ago. Some of the islands are rugged and mountainous; the highest point in the West Indies is Pico Duarte in the Dominican Republic on Hispaniola, which reaches 10,417 feet (3,125 meters). Other island mountains have been worn smooth by rain and wind over many years. The ancient Caribbean Andes mountain range included many volcanoes, and both extinct and active volcanoes are found today on some islands in the Antilles.

A few of the Lesser Antilles are not mountaintop islands. For example, Trinidad and Tobago are part of the continent of South America. Many centuries ago they were separated from the rest of the continent by the formation of the Gulf of Paria. Trinidad and Tobago have the same soil, rocks, and plant and animal life as the nearby Venezuelan coast. The Dutch islands of Aruba, Bonaire, and Curaçao, north of Venezuela, are also geographically related to the South American continent.

Several important island groups that do not belong to the Antilles chain are considered part of the West Indies. The Cayman Islands, south of Cuba, are coral islands formed by colonies of millions of coral polyps. North of Cuba and Hispaniola is the Bahama Islands chain, which includes the Turks and Caicos Islands at its southern end. This chain is also made of coral. The 145 or so islands of Bermuda are located far to the north, off the coast of North Carolina in the United States. The Bermuda Islands are a cluster of coral islands that have formed on top of an isolated undersea mountain peak.

All of these islands share a common West Indian history and culture. The region's total land area is more than 91,000 square miles (236,600 square kilometers). Its total population is about 36 million.

Climate and Weather

Except for Bermuda and the northern Bahamas, all the islands of the West Indies lie between the Tropic of Cancer and the equator. This places them in the tropical zone, where the weather stays warm or hot all year.

The average annual temperature in the West Indies is about 80° Fahrenheit (27° Centigrade). The coolest months are January and February, when it rarely falls below 75° F (24° C). During the hotter summer months, most islands are swept by cool breezes that keep the thermometer from rising above 87° F (30° C).

These cooling winds, which blow steadily from the northeast, are called trade winds because they were used to blow the sailing ships of the colonial trade straight to the islands. The northern and eastern coasts of the islands face the Atlantic Ocean and the trade winds; they are called the "windward" sides. The more sheltered western and southern coasts are called the "leeward" sides. With the exceptions of Havana in Cuba and San Juan in Puerto Rico, most major ports and settlements in the West Indies are along the leeward coasts.

The trade winds also bring rain to the islands. This means that the windward sides of most islands are greener and lusher than the leeward sides. The West Indies receive an average of 65 inches (1,651 millimeters) of rainfall each year. Some islands receive less. Antigua gets about only 44 inches (1,118 mm), and the Turks and Caicos receive a mere 21 inches (533 mm). About 60 inches (1,524 mm) of rain falls on the western or leeward side of Jamaica, but the eastern or windward side, where mountain peaks trap the moisture-laden clouds of the trade winds, receives about 150 inches (3,810 mm). Mountainous Dominica gets more than 120 inches (3,048 mm).

Rainfall in the West Indies follows a seasonal pattern. Most rain falls during the wet season, which lasts from June to October or November. During this season it may rain for part of every day. Little rain falls during the dry season, which occurs during the winter and spring months. Many of the smaller islands have no rivers, and the rivers and streams of the larger islands often dry up during the dry season. As a result, water shortages are a problem, especially on the smaller, flatter islands.

The West Indians deal with drought in various ways. People on Antigua and the Turks and Caicos Islands build large cisterns to catch and store rainwater; the Bahamians and Virgin Islanders dig deep wells to tap buried streams; and the farmers of Jamaica, Cuba, and Hispaniola irrigate their fields during the dry months. The people of Barbados are fortunate; their island has a large freshwater lake, so they have abundant water. On Aruba and on Curaçao in the Netherlands Antilles, income from oil refineries has been used to build plants that distill seawater into drinking water. Such plants are expensive, however, and most West Indian nations cannot afford them.

A greater menace than water shortages confronts the islands every year from July to October. It is the hurricane, a devastating storm of wind and rain that blows in from the Atlantic across the Lesser Antilles, and then usually turns north toward the Greater Antilles and North America. Several hurricanes may strike the West Indies in a single season. Today, modern technology, including satellites to watch storm clouds and computers to predict their movements, is used to warn islanders against hurricanes. Such methods save lives, but hurricanes still cause great damage. Hurricanes David (1979), Allen (1980), Gilbert (1988), Hugo (1989), and Andrew (1993) devastated various islands of the West Indies.

Santo Domingo in the Dominican Republic was devastated by Hurricane David.

Plant and Animal Life

The mountainous areas of the West Indies are thickly forested. Vines, shrubs, and bushes, as well as tropical trees such as mahogany, cedar, greenheart, and mora grow on the mountainsides. Some of these trees are valuable for woodworking and building, but they seldom occur in great quantities. Nearly all of the lowland and many patches of mountainside have been cleared for farming.

The flatter islands and low-lying plains are sparsely covered with pines, palms, scrub oak, cacti, and thornbushes. Many islands are fringed with mangrove swamps (coastal forests of low, twisted trees whose roots are hidden by the sea at high tide). The West Indies are famed for the beauty and variety of their flowers and blossoming trees: the scarlet flamboyant tree, the poinsettia, the hibiscus, the sweet-smelling frangipani, and the bougainvillea.

Many of the colorful birds of South America—toucans, parrots, trogans, flamingos, and hummingbirds—are found in the islands. In addition, some common North American songbirds migrate to the West Indies during the winter months. Native mammals include bats, deer, monkeys, and agouti (small, rabbit-like rodents). Lizards, tortoises, scorpions, centipedes, and insects are numerous, and poi-

The native wildlife of the region includes many small creatures such as lizards, tortoises, and bats.

sonous bushmaster, fer-de-lance, and coral snakes are sometimes found. The sea around the islands is rich with creatures of all kinds, including sharks, flying fish, lobsters, shrimp, and hundreds of species of brilliantly colored, reef-dwelling tropical fish.

Much of the region's plant and animal life, like its human population, has come from other parts of the world. European settlers introduced domestic animals such as chickens, donkeys (widely used for transportation, especially in poorer regions), cattle, pigs, dogs, sheep, and goats. The mongoose (a weasel-like burrowing mammal) was brought from India to kill snakes in the islands; it did the job well, but now some islands have a surplus of mongooses. The mango, one of the most popular fruits of the region, also came from India.

Sugarcane, the economic mainstay of the West Indies for several centuries, was brought by the Spanish, who also imported citrus fruits. Coffee, an important crop on several islands, came from Arabia by way of Brazil. The cocoa and bougainvillea plants were brought from South America; the hibiscus came from China. Spices such as nutmeg and cloves came from the East Indies. Captain William Bligh, the commander of the British ship *Bounty* at the time of its famous mutiny, brought three important food plants to the West Indies from the South Seas: the coconut palm, the breadfruit tree, and the banana plant. All of these "immigrants" are now at home in the West Indies—so much so that it is hard to imagine what the islands were like without them.

Indians and Explorers

The island nations of the West Indies share a common early history, although each country developed separately. Archaeologists (scientists who study the traces of past cultures) believe that the Caribbean region was uninhabited until about 1500 B.C., when its first inhabitants, the hunting and fishing Indians called the Ciboney, arrived from Central or South America.

Between 100 B.C. and 100 A.D., another group of Indians, the Arawak, came to the Lesser Antilles from Venezuela. They spread northward through the island chain, bringing farming skills and the art of pottery. By about 1000 A.D., various Arawak tribes had driven the few surviving Ciboney into remote regions of western Hispaniola and Cuba. Religious ceremonies played an important part in the daily life of the Arawak; among the few objects these farming people left behind are *zemis*, small stone statues of their gods.

A third wave of Indian peoples, the Caribs, moved into the region between 1000 and 1500. They probably came from either Venezuela or the Guyana area of South America. Warfare, not religion, was the center of their culture, and before long they had seized most of the Lesser Antilles. The Arawak were killed or driven to the Greater Antilles, the Bahamas, and Trinidad.

The Ciboney were almost extinct by the time other European explorers and settlers arrived after Columbus's discovery of the region. The Arawak were numerous on the larger islands. They usually greeted the white newcomers peacefully, but they were not treated well in return. The Arawak were killed by the Europeans' firearms or by new diseases such as smallpox. They were forced to labor as slaves on white-owned farms and plantations. By about 1550, the Arawak population of the West Indies had been reduced to small communities in Cuba and Trinidad, and the Europeans began to look elsewhere for forced labor. In a few generations, the surviving Arawak died off or blended with the rest of island society.

Unlike the Arawak, the Caribs fought fiercely against the whites. They were hated and feared by the settlers, who coined the word "cannibalism" from the Carib practice of eating dead enemies. (The Caribs also gave their name to the Caribbean Sea that surrounds the West Indian islands.) The Caribs kept the Europeans from settling some islands, such as Dominica and St. Vincent, for a century or more, but eventually they were nearly wiped out by the superior

The Carib Indians once occupied all of the smaller islands; today they live in Dominica.

weapons and new diseases of the whites. Some Carib and Arawak women had children fathered by white settlers or black slaves, however, and many islanders today have traces of Indian ancestry.

In the 1700s, runaway black slaves joined the Caribs and intermarried with them, forming a people called the black Caribs. One group of black Caribs was shipped by the British from St. Vincent to Central America, where their descendants still speak a version of the old Indian language. The British rounded up the remainder of the surviving Caribs and settled them in a reservation on Dominica. A few hundred Caribs live there today. As recently as 1903, a "Carib war" took place when the Indians revolted against mistreatment by the Dominican police.

The Spanish held almost unchallenged power in the Caribbean for more than a century after Columbus's arrival. At first they sought gold. When the meager supply of gold on Hispaniola and Cuba gave out, the rich gold mines of Mexico and Central and South America lured the explorers and adventurers from the islands. The Spanish introduced cattle-ranching to the Greater Antilles islands. These islands became the bases for expeditions to the Mexican or Central American mainland, then called the Spanish Main. Pirates and privateers (privately owned, armed ships licensed by European governments to attack Spanish shipping) began to prey on Spanish galleons, which were heavily laden with treasure from the mines of the Aztecs and Incas. Piracy would be part of Caribbean life for several centuries.

The Netherlands, Britain, and France began to stake claims to the West Indies in the early 1600s. Spain was unable to defend its colonies in the West Indies because it was busy fighting in Europe and colonizing the mainland. Spain lost the Lesser Antilles and Jamaica as well as one-third of Hispaniola. The West Indies became the scene of conflicting claims, rivalries, and territorial warfare among the European powers, especially Britain and France. Over the next two centuries, many islands changed hands repeatedly as a result of local battles or treaties signed in far-off European palaces.

Also important in the early history of the Caribbean was the buccaneer society. Buccaneers were English, French, Dutch, and Portuguese smugglers and adventurers who were united against Spain and were tolerated by their own governments because they attacked Spanish ships and cities. Sometimes they even accompanied regular troops in battles against the Spanish. The buccaneers operated out of Hispaniola in the early 1600s, but, after helping the British capture Jamaica in 1655, they turned the Jamaican city of Port Royal into a buccaneers' haven; a British writer of the time called it "the richest and wickedest city on earth."

Captain Henry Morgan was the most notorious of the buccaneers. Finally, the actions of the buccaneers became too bold and aggressive, and the European nations began to regard them as out-

The notorious buccaneer Henry Morgan was made lieutenant governor of Jamaica in 1674.

laws and pirates. In 1672, Morgan was sent to England and imprisoned in the Tower of London. After two years, he was allowed to return to the island. In fact, he was made lieutenant governor—on the condition that he stamp out piracy. At about the same time, the British and French buccaneers began to turn against each other, destroying the unity of buccaneer society.

The death blow to buccaneering was the great Jamaican earthquake of 1692. Port Royal slid into the sea, and, according to legend, immense hoards of pirate gold and silver went with it. Many pirates operated in the Caribbean in later years, and legends of hidden strongholds and buried treasure are still heard throughout the West Indies.

The importation of slaves and laborers from distant parts of the world had a strong impact on the West Indies. Slave labor became common in the late 1600s, when the Europeans found that sugarcane was the most profitable crop they could grow on the West

Indian islands. Growing and harvesting the sugarcane required considerable labor, but neither the native Indians nor imported European criminals and political prisoners proved to be good workers. The Europeans thus turned to slaves.

The Spanish had introduced a few black slaves from Africa to their mines and cattle ranches in the 16th century. In the late 17th and 18th centuries, France and England shipped thousands of blacks, mostly from West Africa, to the sugarcane plantations of the islands. Slaves soon outnumbered the whites on most islands. Many African words, beliefs, and customs survived the transatlantic crossing and took root in the New World.

Slave revolts were common, and in one uprising in the late 1700s, the slaves succeeded in seizing control of part of Hispaniola from the French. The colony soon became the republic of Haiti, the first black nation in the New World.

In the 19th century, slavery was abolished in the colonies, and plantation owners were forced to seek labor elsewhere. They brought thousands of laborers from British colonies in India and the East Indies to Trinidad and other islands. Most of these laborers had contracts specifying that they could return to their homelands after ten years or so. But many of them finished their contracts, sent for their families, and stayed to become part of the ethnic mixture of the West Indies.

In the 20th century, independence movements swept colonies all over the world. Many colonies declared or fought for their own national identities. In the Caribbean, a number of the West Indian colonies achieved independence from Great Britain, France, and Spain. The debate over independence continues to be an important political issue in those islands that remain colonies.

Like most of the small farms in the hilly highlands of the larger islands, this tobacco field in Puerto Rico is steep and must be worked by hand.

The Greater Antilles

The Greater Antilles portion of the West Indies consists of the four largest Caribbean islands: Cuba, Hispaniola (divided between the countries of the Dominican Republic and Haiti), Jamaica, and Puerto Rico. Each island's territory includes many smaller islands and tiny cays (pronounced keys) in its offshore waters.

Cuba is the largest of the West Indian islands. Called by the early Spaniards "the pearl of the Antilles," Cuba has an area of 44,218 square miles (114,524 square kilometers) and includes 3,715 small islands and cays. It is 90 miles (144 km) south of Florida and about the same distance north of Jamaica; its closest neighbor, Haiti, is 48 miles (77 km) to the east.

Cuba's capital is the old Spanish port city of Havana, located on the northwestern coast of the main island. Its second largest island, with an area of 849 square miles (2,207 sq km), lies off the main island's southwestern coast. Once called the Isle of Pines, it has been renamed the Isle of Youth because so many young Cubans have settled there.

About one-fourth of the main island is covered with mountains. The valleys, plains, and coastal lowlands of the rest of the island provide rich soil for sugarcane cultivation and cattle pastures. Cuba has several unusual species of tree: the West Indian ebony is rare and valuable; the royal palm, the national tree, reaches heights of 75 feet (23 meters); and the cork palm of the western regions has been called a "living fossil" by scientists—it is a relic of the Cretaceous Period, more than 100 million years ago. Animal life includes two rare species of crocodile and the solenodon, a ratlike insect-eater found nowhere else in the world.

The Cuban people reflect a mixture of Spanish, African, Chinese, and Central American ancestry. Spanish is the national language, and Roman Catholicism is the dominant religion. Santeria, a religious cult that identifies Catholic saints with deities from traditional African religions, is also widely practiced. The island's culture has produced many forms of internationally popular dance music, such as the rhumba, that combine Spanish and African rhythms. Cuba's

Cuba's capital city is Havana, the former Spanish colonial port.

Farms crowd the hills and cliffs of the Virales Valley, Cuba.

well-known musical figures include Gloria Estefan, Adalberto Alvarez, and the group Síntesis.

Education is free in Cuba, and the government provides scholarships to help students with living expenses. A large percentage of the national budget goes toward improving schools and training teachers; the government hopes to make all citizens literate (able to read and write) by the end of the century. The number of students enrolled in school at all levels has risen greatly since the 1950s.

The state also provides free medical care. As elsewhere in the Caribbean, tropical diseases such as malaria and yellow fever, which once struck down many people, have been brought under control. However, economic hardship brought on by the withdrawal of Soviet aid and by U.S. sanctions led to severe health problems from malnutrition in the late 1980s and early 1990s.

Cuba's economy has always been based on agriculture. In colonial times, tobacco and sugarcane were grown on large estates called *latifundios*. Today, sugarcane remains the principal crop, but the government is trying to develop other industries as well. Nickel, chromite, and copper are mined, and the island has deposits of iron ore and manganese. Factories produce food, beverages, shoes, cement, fertilizer, and textiles, but processing sugarcane into sugar and other products (rum, molasses, and a cattle feed called *molascuit*) is the largest industry.

Columbus discovered Cuba and claimed it for Spain during his first voyage. A Spaniard named Diego Velázquez founded the first settlement in 1511. Cuba remained in Spanish hands for almost the next four centuries. In the 1500s, it was the starting point for many expeditions to the Spanish Main. In the 1600s, the colony suffered through hurricanes, diseases, pirates, and battles between rival European powers. Sugarcane cultivation became the backbone of the economy during the 1700s, however, and by 1880 Cuba's sugar industry was the most mechanized and productive in the world.

In 1895, Cuban rebels began a war to seek Cuba's independence from Spain. Backed by the United States, which entered the war in 1898, Cuba won its independence in 1899. U.S. troops remained on the island for several years. After they withdrew in 1902, a series of political parties and leaders fought for control of Cuba. Over the next 50 years, Cuba endured many leaders, many of whom were incompetent or corrupt. In 1958, Fidel Castro overthrew President Fulgencio Batista and established a new government based on Communist principles.

Unhappy with a Communist nation so close to its borders, the United States sponsored an invasion by a group of Cuban exiles. The invaders, who planned to overthrow Castro and form a new government, landed at the Bay of Pigs in 1961. The attempt failed, and relations between the United States and Cuba have been poor ever since—although Castro permitted 120,000 Cubans to emigrate to the U.S. in 1980.

Fidel Castro, head of Cuba's Communist party, seized power in a 1958 coup.

By refusing to allow trade with Cuba, the United States hoped to cause enough hardship on the island to bring down Castro's government. However, aid from the Soviet Union filled the gap. When the Soviet Union collapsed in the late 1980s, this aid was withdrawn. The United States then applied further sanctions. In response to these events, the Cuban economy went into a tailspin that severely lowered the population's health and standard of living. Castro has responded by loosening government control of business and encouraging tourism, leading to some degree of economic recovery.

Dominican Republic

The Dominican Republic occupies the eastern two-thirds of Hispaniola, the second largest island in the West Indies; the other one-third is occupied by Haiti. To the north of Hispaniola is the Atlantic Ocean; to the south, the Caribbean Sea; to the west, Cuba; and to the east, Puerto Rico. Hispaniola is about 600 miles (960 kilometers) southeast of Florida and about half that distance north of South America. The Dominican Republic has an area of 18,704 square miles (48,630 square kilometers). Its capital is Santo Domingo.

The country's landscape is mountainous and rugged. Pico Duarte, in the central mountains of the Dominican Republic, is the highest point in the West Indies 10,417 feet (3,125 meters). The northern and southern ends of the border with Haiti are dry and desert-like. Rolling plains are found in the far southeast.

Although the economy is mainly agricultural, only one-fifth of the land is suitable for cultivation, and just half of that is used for farming. The rest consists of pastures and meadows for cattle grazing. The Dominican Republic possesses one unusual natural resource: high-quality amber (the petrified resin of ancient trees and plants, valued as a gem because of its clear or milky golden color). Local craftspeople make amber jewelry for sale to tourists.

Most Dominicans are *mestizos* (people of mixed race), although there are smaller groups of whites and blacks. A community of rice farmers in the Constanza Valley is descended from Japanese laborers. Spanish is the official language, but many immigrants from the neighboring country of Haiti speak a patois (local language) based on French. Most Dominicans are Roman Catholic, and the church is involved in daily life and politics.

More than half of the population lives in rural areas, the scattered homesteads clustered around stores or churches. Some homes can be reached only on foot or horseback. However, Santo Domingo is growing rapidly as Dominicans and immigrants from other West Indian nations seek jobs in the sugar-processing and textile industries or on the fishing boats.

The first colony in the New World was established in the Dominican Republic by Columbus himself. The entire island remained under Spanish control until the 1600s, when French planters developed a sugarcane industry in the western region. In the late 1700s,

Rafael Trujillo ruled the Dominican Republic with a heavy hand for more than 30 years.

Hispaniola underwent two upheavals: black slaves on the French plantations overthrew their white masters and declared their part of the island independent, and Spain gave up control of the entire island to France after military defeats in Europe.

In 1795, the newly freed Haitian blacks invaded the eastern two-thirds of the island, but were driven back with the aid of the British. This part of the island was returned to Spain in 1809, declared itself independent as the Dominican Republic in 1821, and was overrun by Haitian troops from 1822 to 1844. In 1930, the Dominican Republic came under the power of a strict dictator, Rafael Trujillo. Trujillo improved the economy but violated human and civil rights. His regime ended in 1961 when he was killed by members of his own army. A new, conservative government then seized power.

In 1965, the United States sent troops to the Dominican Republic to quell a revolution against the new government. This caused Cuban President Fidel Castro to protest U.S. involvement in Caribbean affairs. In 1978, a more liberal government came to power in the Dominican elections and some social reforms began. That year marked the country's first transfer of power from one democratically elected president to another. Recent years have brought a gradual trend toward a more open economy and a less restrictive government in the Dominican Republic.

Haiti

Haiti shares the island of Hispaniola with the Dominican Republic. It occupies an area of 10,714 square miles (27,856 square kilometers), or a little more than one-third of the island. Its capital is Port-au-Prince, located in central Haiti along the Gulf of Gonâve. Cap-Haïtien is the major port and city on the northern coast.

The country consists of two large peninsulas, or arms of land, that stretch westward from the central mountains. The Gulf of Gonâve and the fertile Plain of Artibonite lie between these two rugged, sandy peninsulas. Haiti also possesses several offshore islands. The largest is La Gonâve, about 40 miles (64 kilometers) northwest of Port-au-Prince. Another Haitian island, Tortuga, was a buccaneers' stronghold in the 17th century.

Most Haitians live in the countryside. Their scattered family settlements consist of a few wooden houses sheltered by banana or coffee trees and surrounded by mud-brick walls. Since the mid-20th century, however, more people have begun moving to the cities, and Port-au-Prince has grown rapidly. It is now bordered by a semicircle of shanty towns—districts without plumbing or electricity where the very poor live in huts, tents, or primitive shelters made of scrap metal and cardboard. The majority of the shanty dwellers cannot read or write and are unable to find work in the city.

The majority of the population is black, although the minority of mixed-race people has traditionally held the most important jobs in business and government. There are a few whites, mainly of French, German, or Italian descent.

The official language is French, but people everywhere speak Creole, a patois that mixes French with words and grammar rules from the languages of West Africa and the Congo. Although nearly everyone is Roman Catholic, most Haitians also follow the beliefs and practices of a local religion called Voudoun, or Voodoo—a blend of Catholic rituals and traditional African spirit worship. Voudounists believe that a Voudoun priest can cast a spell for good luck or misfortune, or even for death. Secret Voudoun societies are said to control *zombies*, or the "living dead," people who walk around in a daze as though they are sleepwalking. Many believe that zombies are actually enemies whom Voudoun worshippers have injected with strong nerve poisons made from herbs or fish.

Haiti is a poor island. Its few mineral resources include gold, silver, bauxite, and copper, but they occur in quantities too small to be profitably mined. Agriculture is the main economic activity. To clear land for cultivation, Haiti has been stripped of all forest except for a few stands of pine, mahogany, and cedar high in the mountains. Coffee is the main crop and is grown on the mountain slopes. Sugar-

Haitians perform a Voudoun ceremony for an audience. Voudoun is a powerful social and political force as well as a religion.

cane and sisal (a fiber used in rope-making) are grown on the plains, but the fields must be irrigated and water shortages sometimes occur. Overpopulation and poor farming techniques have led to soil erosion and low agricultural productivity in many areas.

Farmers grow rice, corn, peas and beans, fruit, and cassava (a starchy root that can be ground into flour) for their own use. These items make up the average diet throughout the Caribbean, with a little fish, chicken, or goat thrown in. Peppers, onions, and spices are used to flavor food and add variety. Creole cuisine, from the humblest peasant fare to the most elaborate meals served in the luxury hotels, is characterized by the lavish use of seasonings and by dishes in which small amounts of many ingredients are mixed together.

After the 1950s, tourism began to play an important role in Haiti's economy. By the 1970s, it was second only to coffee as a source of income for Haiti. But the nation's tourist industry suffered a harsh blow in the 1980s, when it was discovered that many cases of the deadly disease AIDS (acquired immune deficiency syndrome) had been found in Haitians. Political unrest also contributed to the decline of tourism. Haiti has a long history of political turbulence. In the 1600s, former French pirates established plantations on the western end of the Spanish island of Hispaniola. After a century of fighting with Spain, France officially acquired the region in 1697 and named it Saint Domingue.

A century later, the island's half-million African slaves rose in revolt against their few thousand white owners. Led by a slave called Toussaint Louverture, and later by Jean-Jacques Dessalines and Henri Christophe, the blacks won their independence from France in 1804. They created a new nation with the Arawak Indian name Haiti; then they tried to take over the entire island.

For 20 years, the Haitians fought the Spanish in eastern Hispaniola and fought among one another at home. Various former

(continued on p. 73)

SCENES OF
WEST INDIES

◄ *Flamboyant costumes and*
musical parades are part of
the annual Carnival festival
on Trinidad, Grenada, and
other islands.

◄ *This young Jamaican, swimming in the crystal waters off an island beach, may face an uncertain future in a land troubled by poverty.*

Ⅴ *Early Swedish settlers built this clock tower on St. Barthélemy. Usually called St. Bart's, the small volcanic island is now part of France's overseas territory. It is a popular and stylish vacation spot, noted for fine dining and unspoiled beaches.*

◄ *Tortola is a typical island paradise, seen from the air: Its palm-covered hills, sandy beaches, and blue waters have captivated visitors for centuries. In the picture's center is Road Town, capital of the British Virgin Islands.*

⋏ *St. Mary's Catholic Church, built in 1935, lends the look of an English countryside to Kingston, St. Vincent. Now a self-governing republic, St. Vincent was probably discovered by Columbus but was a British colony for two centuries before becoming independent in 1979. It remains part of the Commonwealth of Nations, headed by Great Britain.*

⋏ *Les Saintes, one of the tiny islands included in the French overseas department of Guadeloupe, is the home of many of Guadeloupe's well-to-do citizens and is a popular weekend and vacation spot for people from the other islands.*

◄ *This landscape in the highlands of Trinidad, with its looming hills, empty road, and tiny houses half-hidden in the lush vegetation, could represent rural life almost anywhere in the West Indies.*

◄ Africans were first brought to the West Indies as slaves on the sugarcane plantations. Sugar remains an important export crop in Cuba, Haiti, the Dominican Republic, and most of the larger islands.

➤ Fishermen in Rock Sound, the Bahamas, bring ashore a day's catch. Tourism and finance dominate the Bahamian economy, but many families in the outlying islands live by fishing and farming.

◄ The colorful harbor of St. George's, the capital of Grenada, was a center of shipbuilding and schooner repair during the colonial era. It remains in the boating business today as the home port of many yachts and fishing vessels.

⋏ *Many food crops have been introduced to the West Indies from other parts of the world, but the beauty of thousands of flowering shrubs and brilliant blooms is the island's own.*

(continued from p. 64)

Toussaint Louverture, leader of Haiti's slave revolt, has been called "the father of Caribbean independence."

slaves claimed power, including Christophe. Although many Haitians turned against him, Christophe reigned as king of Haiti from 1811 until his suicide in 1820.

After Christophe's death, Haiti invaded the Spanish portion of Hispaniola again and occupied it for 20 years. By 1915, Haiti had suffered through a series of rulers, many of whom died at the hands of assassins or in coups. The United States believed this political instability threatened American-owned sugar refineries. To protect American investment, the United States sent Marines to the island in 1915. U.S. forces occupied the island until 1934.

Following the withdrawal of U.S. troops, military councils ruled the country until 1957, when a new leader emerged: François Duvalier, who was called Papa Doc. Elected president for life, Duvalier ruled as an absolute dictator for a quarter of a century. Duvalier used secret police and bands of Voudoun terrorists, known as the Tontons Macoutes (bogeymen), to crush opposition to his rule. When he died in 1971, he was succeeded by his son, Jean-Claude, or Baby Doc. Jean-Claude continued his father's repressive policies until 1986, when the Haitian people rebelled and drove him into exile.

Duvalier's removal was followed by short-lived military governments that further impoverished and terrorized the nation. In 1994, when Jean-Bertrand Aristide—who had been elected president, then removed by a coup—was reinstated, an end to political chaos finally seemed likely. In 1996 Aristide handed over power to another democratically elected president, René García Préval.

Before 1804, Saint Domingue had been the richest colony in the New World. But independence brought poverty to Haiti. Most of the freed slaves refused to work on the large sugar farms. They

Archaeologists have found relics of Indian life, but the native peoples of Haiti no longer exist.

abandoned cash crops in favor of small farms where they grew only enough to feed their families. Although cash crops are now cultivated and a few small industries have been producing toys, perfume oils, and electronic components, most Haitians remain poor. In fact, Haiti is the poorest country in the Western Hemisphere.

Jamaica

Jamaica lies 90 miles (144 kilometers) south of Cuba, between Haiti and the Central American nation of Nicaragua. Columbus, who discovered it in 1494, called it "the fairest isle that eyes have beheld." The Spanish named the island Jamaica, from the Indian name Xaymaca.

Jamaica is a mountainous island, bordered by coastal plains and sandy beaches and cut through with many short, steep rivers. The landscape varies from rain forest in the highlands, dwarf forest on the highest peaks, and desert-like regions in the south. A 500-square-mile (1,300-square-kilometer) region of the interior is known as Cockpit Country—a trackless, largely unexplored area of rugged limestone pits, caves, and hills covered by thick, scrubby brush. The total area is 4,411 square miles (11,424 sq km). The island's capital is Kingston; Montego Bay, Ocho Rios, and Port Antonio are other important towns.

The island's population is almost entirely black or of mixed black and white race. Because Britain ruled the island from 1655 until 1962, English is the official language, although many Jamaicans speak a local dialect that features many African, Spanish, and French words and a unique, rhythmic lilt. Anglicanism is the major religion, but some Christian sects use African rituals, such as drumming and dancing, in their worship.

The Rastafarian religion, which draws on elements of the ancient Ethiopian Christian Church, has become popular among young people. Jamaica's best-known cultural contribution to the modern

Scenic Ocho Rios brings much-needed tourist dollars to Jamaica.

world is probably reggae, a dance music with a syncopated beat. Its lyrics protest social injustices and praise Rastafarianism.

Jamaica's economy depends on three things: agriculture (mostly sugarcane and bananas grown for export), mining bauxite (used in manufacturing aluminum), and tourism. In the late 1970s and early 1980s, reports of racial unrest and high crime rates slowed the flow of tourists. Since then, the government has started a program to educate Jamaicans about the benefits of tourism, and visitors are once again flocking to the island.

Claimed by Spain, Jamaica was the property of the Columbus family during the 1500s. The early Spanish settlers set up cattle ranches. In 1655, Britain captured the island. Black slaves who had worked on Spanish plantations fled to the hills and to Cockpit Country, where they intermarried with the Indians to form what are called the Maroon societies. Later, blacks who escaped from the British also joined the Maroons. These reclusive communities of farmers, hunters, and smugglers kept up an intermittent guerrilla war against the British for several centuries. Their descendants still live in the Maroon district of the Cockpit Country.

In the late 1600s, Jamaica's Port Royal became the capital of buccaneers and pirates in the Caribbean. Over the following century, sugarcane plantations became the economic mainstay of the island. The 1800s saw the abolition of slavery and the beginnings of self-rule. In the mid-1900s, bauxite-mining developed into an important industry. In 1958, Jamaica joined with a group of British West Indian colonies to form the Federation on the West Indies, a unit within the Commonwealth of Nations. Many people hoped that the Federation would pave the way for a unified Caribbean nation, but it broke up in 1962 when Jamaica withdrew and declared its independence.

During the 1970s, Jamaica's government moved toward socialism and established ties with Communist Cuba. But Edward Seaga, elected prime minister in 1980, sought closer relations with the United States. His successor, Michael Manley, continued in this direction even though Manley had initiated the earlier move to socialism. In the 1990s, crime, unemployment, and poverty remained major problems.

Puerto Rico

The easternmost of the Greater Antilles, Puerto Rico lies 1,050 miles (1,680 kilometers) southeast of Miami, between Hispaniola and the Virgin Islands. Its area is 3,435 square miles (8,931 square kilometers). Like Jamaica, it is a mountainous island, with a rugged interior, coastal plains, and desert-like conditions in the southwest. The lush rain forest of El Yunque, in the northeast, has many species of ferns, orchids, and vines. It is part of the Caribbean National Forest park. The small islands of Vieques and Culebra, off the eastern coast, are part of Puerto Rico. The territory's capital is San Juan.

The population is mainly of Spanish or African descent. Many of the *jibaros*, the rural peasants of the interior, have native Indian

The Spanish fort El Morro looms behind a huddle of San Juan houses.

ancestors. Puerto Rico's culture is largely Spanish: most people are Roman Catholics, and Spanish and English are the official languages (everyone speaks Spanish, and most also speak English).

Although their island is poor in minerals, the Puerto Ricans have built an industrial economy that manufactures textiles, plastics, and chemicals. Oil from South America is refined in Puerto Rican plants before being shipped to customers around the world. And tourism is a significant part of the economy (most visitors are from the United States). In addition, many Puerto Ricans work in the U.S. and send home money that helps the island's economy.

Columbus discovered the island in 1493, and 15 years later Ponce de León gave the harbor at San Juan the name Puerto Rico (Spanish for "rich port"), which later became the name of the island. For several centuries, Puerto Rico was Spain's chief military outpost in the Caribbean. The massive fortress of El Morro, overlooking San Juan harbor, held off several attacks by the British and Dutch. During the 1800s, Spain treated San Juan as part of the parent country rather than as a colony.

The United States captured Puerto Rico in the Spanish-American War of 1898, and made the colony a U.S. territory. In 1947, the United States gave Puerto Ricans the right to elect their own gov-

Puerto Rico's Fountain of the Lions is a replica of a famous one in Spain.

ernors. Since then, the U.S. has given the islanders greater control over their own government. Puerto Rico is now a self-governing commonwealth state voluntarily linked to the United States, which administers its defense and foreign relations. A governor and other officials are elected every four years (all adult citizens may vote); Puerto Rico also sends one representative, who cannot vote, to the U.S. House of Representatives.

Some Puerto Ricans feel that their island should become the fifty-first U.S. state; others—including a few small terrorist groups—want it to become entirely independent. Because the island receives much financial aid from the United States in the form of grants and favorable tax laws, most Puerto Ricans seem to feel that its commonwealth status should remain unchanged, at least for now.

Like most people of the Lesser Antilles, this Martiniquais fisherman is of African descent. In addition to West African influences, the Creole culture of the islands has British, French, and East Indian elements.

The Lesser Antilles

The hundreds of islands that make up the Lesser Antilles are organized into more than a dozen states. Some of these countries are among the world's smallest and youngest independent nations. Although Columbus and other Spanish explorers discovered many of these islands, the Spanish influence is not as strong here as in the Greater Antilles. The Lesser Antilles are an ethnic and cultural medley of British, French, African, and East Indian influences.

Anguilla

Anguilla is a 35-square-mile (91-square-kilometer) island, low in elevation and edged with sandy white beaches. It is a dependency of the United Kingdom. Its chief village and administrative center is called The Valley. Several offshore islands, including Dog, Scrub, and Sombrero, are part of Anguilla. A commissioner appointed by the United Kingdom governs the island; the British government is responsible for defense, public services, and the police. The Anguillans elect a House of Assembly to administer local affairs. English is the official language.

Like other British colonies in the West Indies, Anguilla has a population that is mostly black and of African descent. There are also some people of mixed black and white ancestry. The smallest ethnic group is of British descent; most of these people are administrators.

Although water is sometimes scarce on the riverless coral island, the Anguillans manage to grow fruit trees and raise cattle. Fishing is important to the economy. Early British settlers traded the salt from the large salt pans (shallow pools where the sun causes seawater to evaporate, leaving salt behind) along the coast. Although salt is now manufactured more efficiently in large plants elsewhere in the world, Anguilla still exports some sea salt, along with lobsters and livestock. Discovered by Columbus in 1493, the island was not settled by Europeans until 1650, when it became a British colony. In 1882, it was united into a single colony with the British West Indian islands of St. Kitts and Nevis. In 1967, Anguilla withdrew from this union, claiming that St. Kitts's government and police were too domineering. In 1971, it came under direct British control.

Antigua and Barbuda

The islands of Antigua and Barbuda form an independent republic within the Commonwealth of Nations. Their total area, including the neighboring island of Redonda, is 171 square miles (445 square kilometers). The two islands are largely flat and sandy, although volcanic hills rise in western Antigua. There are no rivers, and all the forests of Antigua were cut down long ago to clear land for farms; Barbuda remains forested. The capital is St. John's.

The English-speaking, mostly black, population lives by growing sugarcane and cotton, which are exported to Great Britain. The uninhabited rock of Redonda, 25 miles (40 kilometers) west of Antigua, has phosphate deposits that the government would like to mine. The islanders elect members to a senate and a house of representatives; the Commonwealth is represented by a governor general appointed by Great Britain.

Columbus visited Antigua in 1493, but the ferocity of the Carib Indians discouraged settlement until the first British colony was set up in 1632. It was raided by the French in 1666 but remained in British hands throughout the rest of its history. The British colonized Barbuda in 1628. In 1680, the British monarch gave possession of this 62-square-mile (161-square-kilometer) island to the Codrington family. They held it until the late 1800s, when it was returned to the British crown. The only settlement on the island today is called Codrington, after the family that owned it for two centuries.

Antigua and Barbuda were joined into a single colony under British administration in the late 1800s. The islands were part of the short-lived Federation of the West Indies from 1958 to 1962. They gained full independence as a single nation in 1981.

Barbados

The most British of the Caribbean islands, Barbados is sometimes called "Little England." Examples of English customs are found throughout the island: cricket is the most popular sport; the harbor officials wear uniforms like those worn centuries ago by members

Centuries of pounding by the surf turns coral and limestone into powdery sand.

of the British Royal Navy; and afternoon tea is a daily ritual. The island was a British colony for 350 years. It is the only Caribbean island that never changed hands or suffered an attack from a rival nation after its first settlement.

The Spanish were the first Europeans in Barbados. During the 1500s, they raided the island and captured Indians to serve as slaves on Hispaniola. By 1550, the Indian population had been wiped out, and the Spanish lost interest in the island. The first settlers, the British, arrived in the 1620s.

During the 1700s, the colonists brought many slaves from Africa to work on the huge sugarcane plantations. After the British abolished slavery in 1834, the island's economy declined while its population increased (today Barbados has one of the highest population densities of the Caribbean region—1,565 people per square mile, or 605 per square kilometer).

Riots broke out in Barbados in 1937, because the Bajuns (the local name for the people of Barbados) believed that Great Britain was ignoring their economic plight and their desire for increased self-government. Over the next few decades, the British granted the Bajuns more civil rights and a greater voice in their own government. Barbados achieved independence in 1966.

After the United States sent troops to Grenada in 1983, some Barbadians feared further U.S. involvement in Caribbean affairs.

Barbados is a dry, generally flat island. Sugarcane is the main agricultural product. Most farmland is owned by corporations or large landowners, so few of the peasant (poor, small-scale) farmers own their own property. Many of them live in tenantries—clusters of wooden homes, called chattel houses, on the borders of the large estates. The tenants usually own these houses but rent the ground on which they stand; the farmer can move his house on a cart or truck if he goes to work on another estate.

Tourism is now the largest part of the of the Barbadian economy. Travelers flock to the white beaches and colorful coral reefs that surround the island. Construction and other industries that support tourism also contribute to the economy.

Dominica

The mountainous, forested island of Dominica covers 290 square miles (754 square kilometers). A former British dependency, it lies between the two French islands of Guadeloupe and Martinique. The capital and chief port is Roseau.

The rugged island of Dominica is of volcanic origin. Signs of volcanic activity remain in its many *solfaratas* (fissures in the ground from which hot gases spew forth), its hot springs, and the Boiling Lake in the southern part of the island, whose waters are heated by escaping gases.

The people of Dominica are mainly black or of mixed black and white race, with smaller groups of Europeans and Syrians. In a reservation on Dominica, live several hundred Carib Indians, the largest group of Caribs to preserve their ethnic identity into the 20th century. Although English is Dominica's official language, most people speak and understand a French patois.

Tourism and agriculture are the main economic activities, and limes, bananas, and sugarcane are the principal crops. Fishing also contributes to the economy and the local diet. Some parts of the island have stands of hardwood trees—ebony, mahogany, and others—that are the basis for the island's small lumber industry. Dominica's economy has improved in recent years, as it has moved toward tourism and away from dependence on agriculture, especially sugar, which regularly suffers from hurricanes and drought.

Dominica was first sighted by Columbus in November of 1493. The Spanish showed little interest in the island because of the fierce Caribs and the island's lack of mineral resources. The French settled the island in 1632. The island changed hands between France and Britain many times until the British took control in 1783. From 1883 to 1940, it was part of the British Leeward Islands colony (a cluster of British possessions in the northern part of the Lesser Antilles). From 1958 to 1962, Dominica belonged to the Federation of the West Indies. It returned to direct British control after the federation broke up, and it achieved independence in 1978.

Grenada

Grenada is sometimes called the "Isle of Spice," because of the pepper, cloves, cinnamon, and nutmeg that thrive on the island. British and French planters brought the spices to Grenada from the East Indies. The island also has valuable hardwood trees, including the blue mahoe and the saman. Small mona monkeys, whose ancestors were brought as pets by slaves from West Africa, clamber among tree branches.

The steep, green, hilly island covers 133 square miles (344 square kilometers). The small island of Carriacou, to the northeast, is a dependency of Grenada. The capital, St. George's, has a fine natural harbor. Rows of pastel houses climb up the hillsides behind the harbor. The waterfront of St. George's is called the Carenage, because many island schooners used to be careened there (towed up onto the sand so that their hulls could be cleaned or repaired). Today,

Although proud of their African cultural heritage, most Grenadians are Christians and worship in Western-style churches like this one in St. George's.

St. George's is one of the Caribbean's main ports for yachts and for boats that can be chartered for deep-sea-fishing.

Like the Dominicans, the Grenadians speak both English (the official language) and a French patois. The two languages are the legacy of several centuries of alternating British and French rule. Most Grenadians are black or of mixed race. Less than three percent of the remaining population is descended from East Indian laborers or European landowners. Agriculture and tourism are Grenada's main sources of income.

Columbus sighted Grenada in 1498, but the Carib Indians drove off attempts at settlement. In 1650, French colonists from Martinique bought the island from a Carib chieftain for some beads, hatchets, and brandy. Throughout the 1700s, the French and the British fought for control of the island. In 1783, the British received the island from France under the Treaty of Versailles. From 1885 to 1958, it was the headquarters of the British Windward Islands colony (a cluster of British possessions in the southern part of the Lesser Antilles). From 1958 to 1962, it belonged to the Federation of the West Indies.

A brief but bloody civil war in Grenada drew the world's attention and led to occupation by U.S. troops.

Grenada became an independent nation and a member of the United Nations in 1974, but its government, led by the eccentric and authoritarian prime minister Eric Gairy, was overthrown in 1979. The new leader, Maurice Bishop, suspended the constitution to establish a Socialist state, but he in turn was overthrown by a military coup in 1983.

When Bishop was ousted, the United States invaded the island, officially to protect Americans studying at the medical school there. However, the United States was primarily interested in preventing the Socialists from regaining power. The constitution was restored and new elections held in 1984. U.S. troops withdrew the following year. Since then, Grenada's government has been stable. The country, like many other West Indian nations, is moving its economy away from agriculture and toward tourism.

Guadeloupe

Guadeloupe is an island group in the eastern Caribbean Sea that covers a total of 687 square miles (1,786 square kilometers). It is an overseas department, or administrative district, of France. (A department is much like a state of the United States.) The two main islands that make up Guadeloupe are Basse-Terre and Grande-Terre. Two small islands about 150 miles (240 km) to the northwest are also part of Guadeloupe. One is St. Barthélemy (called St. Barts), which was purchased from Sweden in 1877. The other is St. Martin, which shares the island of Saint Martin with Sint Maarten, a territory of the Netherlands Antilles. Guadeloupe's capital is Basse-Terre, on the island of the same name, but its largest city is Point-à-Pitre, which is located on the island of Grande-Terre.

Basse-Terre is hilly and thickly forested. It has many volcanic mountains, including the volcanic Soufrière Mountain, which erupted in 1976. St. Martin and St. Bart's are also hilly volcanic islands. All three are noted for their beaches of fine black sand. The sand is black because it has been ground from volcanic lava by the wind and waves. Grande-Terre and the three smaller Guadeloupéen islands to the south—Marie-Galante, Les Saintes, and La Désirade—are composed mostly of coral. They are low, flat, sandy, and dry.

The majority of the population is Creole, mostly black or of mixed black and white race. Most of the white citizens are French, and live on Les Saintes. A small but economically important population of Syrian and Asian descent operates many of Guadeloupe's stores and small businesses. All Guadeloupéens are citizens of France and are represented in the French legislature by five elected members. The islanders also elect a 36-member council for local government. French is the language of business, education, and government, but the local Creole language that is spoken by most islanders also has been made an official language.

Sugarcane, bananas. and vegetables are Guadeloupe's main export crops. Agriculture is less important to the economy than tourism and grants from France. There is almost no industry, although government planners hope to introduce manufacturing to Basse-Terre and Grande-Terre.

Columbus visited the two main islands in 1493. The Spanish tried three times to establish settlements, but the native Carib Indians held them off. Finally, in the 1620s, the Spanish established a foothold on the coast, but were driven out by aggressive French traders. In 1674, Guadeloupe became French property and was considered a dependency of the nearby French colony of Martinique.

Except for brief periods of invasion and attack by the British in the late 1700s and early 1800s, the islands remained under French control. In 1775, Guadeloupe became a single French colony and was separated from Martinique.

In 1946, as a reward for Guadeloupe's loyalty to the Free French (anti-German) forces during World War II, the island received department status. Since then, however, some Guadeloupéens have spoken out in favor of complete independence, even though the island is not economically self-sufficient. Pro-independence groups have carried out bombings in Paris and elsewhere in attempts to force a separation between France and Guadeloupe, but the islands' financial reliance on the parent country makes independence in the near future seem unlikely.

Martinique

Like Guadeloupe, Martinique is an overseas department of France. Its people—predominantly black and mixed race—are French citizens. They send representatives to the national government in France and elect a council that administers local affairs. French is the official language, but Creole is commonly spoken at home and in the markets. The capital is Fort-de-France.

The 431-square-mile (1,121-square-kilometer) island is rugged, mountainous, and volcanic. Mont Pelée, the island's highest point, is an active volcano that rises to 4,583 feet (1,375 meters) in the north. In 1902, it erupted, burying the town of Saint Pierre under a blanket of lava and ash, killing more than 30,000 people. Steep cliffs form Martinique's northern coastline; coral reefs surround the island. The island's beaches are a mixture of powdery white coral sand and fine black volcanic sand.

The coconut palm tree originated in the South Seas and was brought to the Caribbean by Captain William Bligh.

Martinique is one of the most fertile islands in the West Indies, with many kinds of luxuriant tropical vegetation. The island's name is probably a version of the Indian name Madiana (meaning "Island of Flowers"), which Columbus heard the Caribs use when he landed on the island in 1502. Today, its fertile soil is the basis of Martinique's agricultural economy. Sugar, alcohol, and bananas are the main exports.

Tourism has increased since the 1960s, and Fort-de-France has a small oil refinery. Other industries include cement-making, food-processing, and pottery-making. Despite these new industries, Martinique remains an extremely poor, crowded island, and it relies heavily on aid from France and international development funds.

Columbus first landed on Martinique in 1502, but he had already sighted the island in 1493. The Spanish did not stake their claim to the island because it had no gold, so it was left for the French to establish the first European settlement on the island in 1635. In 1674, Martinique became a colony of France; over the next century and a half, it endured many attacks by the British and several short periods of British rule.

By the 18th century, a plantation economy had developed, and many thousands of Africans were imported to work as slaves in the sugarcane fields. The slaves rose up three times—the last time in

Joséphine de Beauharnais, born in Martinique, married Napoléon Bonaparte and became empress of France.

1822—but the uprisings were quelled by troops. After slavery was abolished in 1848, most of the former slaves refused to work on the plantations, and the economy suffered.

After World War II, Martinique became a dependency of France. During the 1960s and 1970s, however, the independence movement gained strength. One of its early leaders was Aimé Césaire, a Martiniquais politician and a noted philosopher and poet.

Today, Martinique's separatists (people who want complete independence from France) seem fewer and less determined than those of neighboring Guadeloupe. Furthermore, the island's economic problems, including the intermittent ravages of hurricanes, stand in the way of independence. France has promised, however, to help the island become economically self-sufficient, which would help make independence a possibility.

Montserrat

Montserrat is a 39-square-mile (101-square-kilometer) volcanic island southwest of Antigua. A colony of the United Kingdom, it is noted for the Irish elements in its culture. Irish names, folklore, and architecture are the legacy of the many settlers who came to the island from Ireland and Virginia during the 1600s. The capital, Plymouth, has been compared to an Irish village.

Columbus sighted the island in 1493 and named it after a Spanish monastery. Sir Thomas Warner, an Englishman, led the first band of English and Irish settlers to Montserrat in 1632. The early colonists battled attacks from the Caribs, who were defeated by the end of the 1600s, and from the French, who captured the island several times before the Treaty of Versailles restored the island to Britain in 1783. Montserrat was part of the British Leeward Islands colony from 1871 to 1956; from 1958 to 1962, it was part of the Federation of the West Indies. Since 1962, it has been under direct British control.

After the abolition of slavery in 1834, the Montserrat Company was organized to sell small farms carved out of the abandoned sugarcane estates. Limes and cotton became important crops for export. By the 1980s, these crops were supplemented by small-scale industries that turned out plastic bags, textiles, and electronic appliances for sale abroad. Tourism also began contributing to the economy.

Politically, from the late 1970s through the mid-1990s, the dominant political issue was independence, favored by a minority. However, politics was overshadowed by a long-term natural disaster. In 1995, the previously dormant Soufrière Hills volcano began eruptions that led to the evacuation of two-thirds of the population.

Netherlands Antilles and Aruba

The Netherlands Antilles and Aruba are all that remain of Dutch colonial power in the Caribbean. They were a single colony until 1986, when Aruba separated from the other islands. Today, both colonies are part of the Kingdom of the Netherlands, but they are responsible for their own internal government.

The Netherlands Antilles consists of two groups of islands about 500 miles (800 kilometers) apart. The larger islands—Bonaire and Curaçao—lie off the coast of Venezuela. Aruba lies close by. Low, dry, and sandy, these three islands are surrounded by magnificent coral reefs rich with sea life. The capital of the Netherlands Antilles, Willemstad, is on Curaçao.

Farther north are the three small, mountainous islands of the Netherlands Antilles: St. Eustatius (sometimes called Statia), Saba, and Sint Maarten (the southern part of this island also contains the French dependency of St. Martin).

The population of all these islands, especially the larger, southern islands, is an ethnic melting pot. People of African, Spanish, Dutch, Portuguese, American Indian, Chinese, East Indian, and South American ancestry are found here. Many people are of mixed race. Dutch is the official language, but most people also speak Spanish, English, or Papiamento, a local language that mixes Spanish with African, Dutch, and Portuguese.

The Netherlands Antilles and Aruba have higher standards of health, education, and economic well-being than any other Caribbean islands. The prosperity is due in part to the oil refineries on the southern islands. Oil from the vast oilfields under Venezuela's Lake Maracaibo is brought to the islands to be refined.

Tourism is the second most important economic activity. The northern islands are considered picturesque tropical paradises, while the southern islands appeal to scuba divers eager to explore their coral reefs and the wrecked ships that lie offshore.

*Refineries in the
Netherlands Antilles
process crude petroleum
from Venezuelan
oilfields.*

Farmers throughout the islands produce fruits and vegetables for local use. Aloes and small oranges are also grown, mainly for export. Aloes are made into medicinal products, and the small oranges are made into a flavored liqueur called Curaçao.

Spanish mariners discovered the southern islands in the 1490s and quickly exterminated most of the native Indians. In the 1600s, the Dutch took control of the islands and built a prosperous economy based on farming, smuggling, and slave-trading. In 1648, the Dutch and French divided the island of Saint Maarten into Sint Maarten and St. Martin; the northern portion obtained by the Dutch, Saint Maarten, was smaller, but it contained valuable salt deposits. Saba, settled by the Dutch at about the same time, was a buccaneer stronghold. St. Eustatius was one of the biggest slave markets in the New World until 1781, when the British attacked and destroyed most of its capital city, Oranjestad.

The islands remained Dutch colonies until 1954, when the government of the Netherlands united the six islands into one group.

At that time the island group—or federation—became part of the Kingdom of the Netherlands, with a local legislature and council of ministers and a governor appointed by the Dutch monarch. In 1986, Aruba separated from the federation, although it remains under Dutch control. Aruba asked to receive full independence from the Netherlands by 1996 but later withdrew the request. The Netherlands has agreed that independence for all the islands is inevitable, but has maintained that the other five should remain united as the Netherlands Antilles until they are granted independence.

St. Kitts and Nevis

The independent, democratic nation of St. Kitts and Nevis (pronounced NEE-vis) consists of two islands with a combined area of 101 square miles (263 square kilometers). The capital is the town of Basseterre on St. Kitts. The islands' soil is volcanic, well watered, and fertile.

The people, mostly blacks or of mixed black and white race, speak English. They elect their own parliament and prime minister. Most people live by cultivating sugarcane and cotton. Industry consists of a few small factories that produce shoes, textiles, and electronic equipment for export. The tourist industry is beginning to grow, although there is a shortage of hotels.

Columbus sighted the islands in 1493, but the warlike Caribs discouraged settlement. The British established a colony on St. Kitts in 1623. Five years later, the British also settled Nevis. Trade and agriculture helped Nevis to flourish. St. Kitts changed hands several times between the British and French, which slowed its economic growth.

In 1882, the British made St. Kitts and Nevis and Anguilla a federation, or single British colony. Anguilla withdrew from this federation in 1967. In 1983, St. Kitts and Nevis became an independent nation within the Commonwealth of Nations.

St. Lucia

St. Lucia is a wooded, hilly island of volcanic origin, with an area of 238 square miles (616 square kilometers). Its capital is Castries.

The majority of St. Lucians are black or of mixed race; others are white or East Indian. St. Lucia's economy is based on agriculture (mainly bananas) and tourism, but neither produces enough income to give the island a comfortable standard of living. Industry is growing slowly, and St. Lucia's leaders hope to increase the island's revenues from tourism and oil-refining in the coming years.

St. Lucia was discovered around 1500, possibly by Columbus. The island was the sight of bitter territorial rivalry between the British and French. The first successful settlers were the French, but the island changed hands fourteen times before Britain gained control in 1814. The population continues to show strong traces of the French influence: Roman Catholicism is the dominant religion, and the common language is a French-based Creole dialect. English is the official language, however.

From 1838 to 1885, St. Lucia was part of the British Windward Islands colony. It joined the short-lived Federation of the West Indies in 1958 and became a state voluntarily associated with the United Kingdom in 1967. It achieved independence in 1979 and became a member of the Commonwealth of Nations.

Twin peaks called the Two Pitons in St. Lucia are the cores of eroded volcanoes.

St. Vincent and the Grenadines

St. Vincent is a 150-square-mile (390-square-kilometer) independent republic within the Commonwealth of Nations. St. Vincent's territory consists of the island of St. Vincent and several dozen, much smaller islands known as the Grenadines, which stretch southward from St. Vincent toward Grenada. The larger Grenadines are Bequia, Canouan, Mayreau, Mustique (famous as the vacation island of the British royal family), and Union. The capital is Kingstown, on St. Vincent.

Columbus visited St. Vincent on his third voyage to the New World in 1498. The first non-Indian settlers were African slaves who were shipwrecked on the island in 1673. The French and British fought over St. Vincent during the mid-1700s, but the British won control of the island in 1783.

With the help of guns and money from the French in Martinique, the native Caribs revolted against British rule in 1795. British troops quelled the revolt, and the Indians were shipped to the coast of Honduras, where their descendants live today.

Throughout the 1800s, St. Vincent's plantations produced sugarcane. The first plantation laborers were black slaves; after slavery was abolished later in the century, they were followed by East Indian contract laborers. Today, the nation's population is mostly black or mixed race, but a significant number are of East Indian descent. There are also a few whites.

Most islanders are farmers. The main crops are sugarcane and arrowroot (a starchy substance used in baby food); St. Vincent is the world's largest exporter of arrowroot, most of which is sold to the United States. Tourism is growing slowly.

St. Vincent was a member of the Federation of the West Indies from 1958 to 1962. In 1969, it became a state associated with the United Kingdom and, in 1979, joined with the Grenadines as an independent nation. Its first year of independence was marred by a major eruption of the volcano Soufrière, followed the next year by Hurricane Allen. These natural disasters have hindered the development of the nation's economy.

Trinidad and Tobago

Trinidad and Tobago are the southernmost islands in the Antilles island chain. The two islands have an area of 1,980 square miles (5,148 square kilometers). The capital is Port-of-Spain on Trinidad.

Trinidad is the larger island. It is hilly, green, and humid. Pitch Lake, in the southwest, is the world's largest source of naturally occurring asphalt. The British explorer Sir Walter Raleigh discovered the lake in 1595 and used tar from it to patch the hulls of his ships.

Tobago, 21 miles (34 km) to the northeast of Trinidad, is less densely populated than Trinidad. It has several small towns and one city, Scarborough. Little Tobago, just off Tobago's northern coast, is sometimes called Bird of Paradise Island, because it has become a sanctuary for the tropical bird of paradise, an endangered species in its native New Guinea.

Trinidad's population includes many ethnic groups that follow a variety of lifestyles. Most workers on the sugarcane plantations of the central plains are of East Indian descent. They live in villages made up of large, extended families and observe the festivals and rituals of the Hindu religion. In mountain villages, however, the people are of African descent and tend to work on small family farms. Most are Christians. Some Christian sects have incorporated African religious practices, including dancing, drumming, and a belief in spirit possession.

Spanish, French, East Indian, African, English, Dutch, Portuguese, and Arawak cultures have contributed to Trinidad's ethnic mix. English is the official language, but three different Creole languages—one based on French, one based on Spanish, and one called

Trinidad English—are also spoken. The East Indians speak Hindi and Urdu, two of the many languages of India.

Trinidad and Tobago have long been poor islands, and many people are unemployed. In recent years, the nation's income has increased with the development of Trinidad's oil and gas fields. Unemployment is less severe than during the 1970s, and the government hopes that industrial development will continue. Most Trinidadians and Tobagans survive by fishing or by growing a few vegetables and fruit trees. The chief export crops are sugar, cocoa, and coffee.

Trinidad and Tobago are just beginning to promote tourism, which could become a major part of the economy. Tobago and northwestern Trinidad attract most of the country's tourists. Many visitors come to enjoy Carnival, the annual week-long festival of music, dancing, and parades that takes place in the early spring. Carnival is the best time to hear steel-band and calypso music, for which Trinidad is famous. The country's many musicians improvise witty, rhythmic dance music, and they are skilled at fashioning instruments out of scrap material (for example, steel drums made of old rain barrels and car parts).

Columbus discovered Trinidad and Tobago in 1498. Spain made Trinidad a crown colony in the 1500s, but it never established a

The Jama Masjid Mosque in Trinidad reflects the Asian heritage of the island's Muslim population.

A high point of Trinidad's annual Carnival is the crowning of the King and Queen of Calypso.

strong settlement there. Britain, Holland, and France tried to claim both Trinidad and Tobago during the 1700s. In 1797, Britain acquired Trinidad; Tobago was obtained five years later. The two were joined into a single colony in 1889.

After winning independence from Britain in 1962, the new nation faced the problems of poverty and unemployment. Rioting and social unrest followed independence, and Prime Minister Eric Williams was forced to declare martial law to end them. Martial law was lifted in 1971.

In 1976, the country adopted a new constitution and became a republic, with an elected president as the formal head of state. The prime minister, however, still functions as the true head of government. In recent years, the government has tried to move the economy away from strict dependence on petroleum. Natural gas has become increasingly important, as has tourism.

Virgin Islands

The northernmost islands in the Lesser Antilles are the Virgin Islands. The 100 small islands and cays that make up the Virgin Islands are territories of the United States and Great Britain. Located just east of Puerto Rico, they have a total area of 192 square miles (497 square kilometers). Claimed by Spain in the 1500s but never settled as a colony, the islands were haunted by pirates and buccaneers who needed hideouts. They were left undeveloped until modern times.

The Virgin Islands enjoy a climate that many people describe as perfect: warmed by the sun year-round, untroubled by humidity, and cooled by the trade winds. The landscape ranges from craggy hills to wide, unspoiled beaches, from rolling plains to patches of forest, and from rocky coasts to quiet lagoons circled with coral reefs. The least attractive feature of the islands is the scarcity of fresh water. Every house or building has a tank on its roof to catch rainwater, which is then stored in underground tanks. Fresh water is so precious that seawater is used for plumbing and fire-fighting.

Almost the entire population is black and of African descent. In recent years, a few Puerto Ricans and North Americans have made their homes in the Virgin Islands. English is the official language of all the Virgin Islands, but most islanders speak a musical Creole dialect based on English that is sometimes called Calypso language.

The British Virgin Islands, a colony of Great Britain, are the eastern half of the Virgin Islands group. The colony includes four large islands—Tortola, Anegada, Virgin Gorda, and Jost Van Dyke—and 32 small ones, many of them uninhabited. The capital and largest settlement is Road Town on Tortola. The British Virgin Islands have been under British control since 1666, when settlers from England ignored Spanish claims to the islands and evicted Dutch buccaneers.

Today, tourism accounts for half of the British Virgin Islands' income; sugarcane, rum, fish, and charcoal are important exports. Economic aid from Britain is also important to the economy. The islanders elect a legislative council, and the British government appoints a governor and an executive council. Unlike the citizens of other colonies in the West Indies, the people of the British Virgin Islands seem happy with their colonial status and have no desire for

The United States bought part of the Virgin Islands in 1917. This is the police station in Christiansted, St. Croix.

independence, probably because they know that their economy would crumble without help from Great Britain.

The U.S. Virgin Islands, which make up the western half of the group, consists of the large islands of St. Croix, St. Thomas, and St. John, as well as many small islets and cays. The capital is Charlotte Amalie on St. Thomas. These islands were settled by Denmark in the 1600s and were called the Danish West Indies until 1917, when the United States bought them. The Scandinavian architecture of many buildings, especially those in Charlotte Amalie, reflects Danish influence.

The islands are administered by the U.S. Department of the Interior. The islanders elect their own governor and a 15-member legislature. The islands are not self-supporting; they receive large financial grants from the United States. The islanders have expressed little interest in independence.

Tourism is the most important part of the economy. Small industries, such as the manufacture of watches, textiles, and medicines have also been developed, and St. Croix has a large oil refinery and an aluminum-processing plant. As a result of these industries and U.S. aid, many islanders enjoy higher incomes than other Caribbean islanders.

This 13-foot-tall tapestry, woven for King Louis XV of France, displays the native people, trees, birds, and fruits of the New World.

Other Islands

A few islands that are not part of the Antilles island chain are considered to be part of the West Indies because their culture and history are West Indian. They are the Bahamas Islands, east of Florida and north of Cuba and Hispaniola; Bermuda, off the coast of North Carolina in the North Atlantic Ocean; the Turks and Caicos Islands, which are really the southern part of the Bahamas chain; and the Cayman Islands, south of Cuba and northwest of Jamaica.

The Bahamas, formerly a British colony, is now an independent nation within the Commonwealth of Nations. The country's name comes from the Spanish word *bajamar*, meaning "shallow water." It is a 760-mile-long (1,223-kilometers-long) maze of 700 islands, cays, and more than 2,400 low, barren rocks that rise above the warm, reef-filled waters. The total land area of the islands is 5,382 square miles (13,939 square kilometers). Fewer than 30 of the islands are inhabited.

The capital is Nassau, which is located on the island of New Providence. Two-thirds of the total population live on New Providence. Other large islands are Grand Bahama (which has the cities of Freeport and West End), Andros, and Eleuthra. The urban centers

The larger islands of the Bahamas have modern roads and bridges; some of the smaller islands, however, remain undeveloped and isolated.

and many resorts are devoted to tourism, the basis of the economy, but people in remote areas live by fishing and farming.

The islands are generally low, sandy, and dry, although sea pines, palms, and flowering bushes are abundant. The year-round warm climate, the gambling casinos, and the hundreds of beaches have made the Bahamas a popular vacation spot. Its location has made it especially popular with North Americans. Visitors can fly from New York to Freeport in about 3 hours.

The population is mostly black, descended from Africans who were brought to the islands as slaves. The British began to settle in the Bahamas in the mid-1600s, and as a result, the country's language and culture are British. Today, people from Haiti and other West Indian islands are flocking to the Bahamas in search of jobs in the tourist industry, bringing their diverse cultures and languages.

During the late 1600s, the islands were bases for pirates, who raided ships throughout the Caribbean. By 1717, they had come under British control, and Woodes Rogers, the first British-appointed governor, soon removed the pirates. The islands' first representative

Tourism got its start in luxury hotels built by the British.

assembly met in 1729, and the Bahamians gradually acquired greater control of their local affairs over the next two centuries. The Bahamas became fully independent in 1973. The head of the government is the prime minister, who is a member of the legislative House of Assembly; the Assembly members are elected by adult Bahamians. The Commonwealth is represented by a governor general.

Bermuda

This self-governing British colony consists of about 150 islands and rock formations. One hundred and twenty of them are named, but only 20 are inhabited. The country's total area is 20 square miles (52 square kilometers). Bermuda's capital is Hamilton, and its only other major settlement is St. George.

The country's main island is made of coral reef laid down on top of an undersea mountain. Bermuda is one of the world's most northerly coral formations (coral is usually found only in the tropical zone). Its beaches are famous for their pinkish coral sand. The islands are slightly hilly, with many unusual rock formations carved over the centuries by the wind and the waves. Flowers, trees, and

Although north of the tropical zone, Bermuda is encircled by coral.

bushes thrive in the sandy soil and the warm, temperate climate. Birds and sea life are abundant, but Bermuda has no native mammals and only one reptile, a harmless lizard.

Like the Bahamians, the Bermudians are English-speaking blacks of African descent. The remainder of the population consists of whites descended from British settlers or 19th-century Portuguese laborers. Bermuda's economy is based on tourism and on the rent paid by the United States for its military stations. Fruits, vegetables, and fish are harvested on the islands, but additional food must be imported to feed the colony's people. The chief export is Easter lilies, of which Bermuda is the world's largest producer.

A British-appointed governor is responsible for Bermuda's finance, foreign affairs, police, and defense. The colony's local parliament has two houses: a Senate (made up of 11 appointed members) and an elected 40-member House of Assembly, which administers local government.

Spanish navigator Juan de Bermúdez may have discovered the islands that bear his name sometime in the early 1500s. They remained uninhabited until a party of British settlers, bound for America, was shipwrecked there in 1609. The British Virginia Colony acquired a charter to colonize the islands, and the settlement grew. Unlike many of the West Indian islands, Bermuda never had a flourishing sugar industry. Its most prosperous trades were smuggling and privateering, blockade-running during the American Civil War, and rum-running during the Prohibition Era in the United States (from 1920 until 1933).

Tourism is now the backbone of the economy. In fact, some people say that the tourist industry began in Bermuda, when a British princess visited the islands. The Princess Hotel was built in her honor, and other travelers and vacationers decided to follow in her footsteps.

Tourists who arrive in cruise ships may tour the island on motor scooters.

Since the late 1960s, Bermuda has experienced racial and economic tensions because much of the colony's money and power is held by a few, mostly white, people. In addition, some younger Bermudians would like the colony to become independent. The pro-independence voices, however, are in the minority; most Bermudians fear that a change in their status would disturb the profitable tourist trade.

Cayman Islands

The British colony of the Cayman Islands consists of Grand Cayman, Little Cayman, and Cayman Brac. The colony's name comes from the *caiman*, a Caribbean species of crocodile that once thrived on the islands but is now extinct there (it still lives in other parts of the Caribbean, but it is an endangered species). Located about 180 miles (288 kilometers) northwest of Jamaica, the Caymans have a combined area of 102 square miles (265 square kilometers). The capital is George Town, on Grand Cayman.

Low-lying, sandy, and enclosed by coral reefs, the Caymans have few natural resources. Tourists, especially scuba divers, have been attracted to the islands because the surrounding waters are rich in fish, coral, and other undersea life. In addition, divers can explore wrecks and swim to the edge of the Cayman Trench, a 19,000-foot (5,700-meter) deep gash in the sea floor south of the islands.

The islands' population is almost evenly divided between whites and blacks. Many residents make their living catching or farming sea turtles and exporting turtle meat, oil, or shell. (In 1979, the United States banned imports of turtle products because of fears that the sea turtles might become extinct.) Many of the islanders also receive money sent home by men who work for the merchant shipping fleets of many nations.

Columbus sighted the Caymans during his last voyage to the West Indies in 1503. Because they were far from the regular shipping lanes and had no valuable resources, they remained uninhabited until the 1700s, when a few British settlers arrived. Many pirates, including Captain Henry Morgan, built strongholds in the Caymans in the 1600s and early 1700s. In 1877, Britain unified the three islands into a single colony. A constitution adopted in 1972 gave the Cayman Islanders self-government in most internal affairs.

Turks and Caicos Islands

The southern extension of the Bahamas archipelago is called the Turks and Caicos Islands. Covering 193 square miles (502 square kilometers), these two groups of islands are a British colony. Grand Turk and Salt Cay are the only two inhabited islands in the Turks

Salt from "mines" like this once dominated the Turks and Caicos economy; today tourism is the main source of revenue.

group; the other six Turks islands are visited from time to time by fishermen or by villagers gathering salt from natural salt pans. The Caicos group is 22 miles (35 km) to the northwest and consists of six inhabited islands and many smaller cays. Grand Turk, on the island of the same name, is the colony's chief town and administrative center.

The islands may have gotten their names from the Turk's head cactus, which grows throughout the colony and has red flowers that look like a fez (a Turkish hat), and from the Spanish word *cayos* (cay). Most of the people are blacks of African descent. English is the official language, but some Creole dialects are spoken. The islanders elect an assembly, headed by the British-appointed governor, to administer local government.

Ponce de León visited the West Indies before seeking the "fountain of youth" in Florida.

For many years, salt was the islands' main export. Today, however, most of the salt-producing operations have gone out of business. The Turks and Caicos export some fish—chiefly lobsters, crayfish, and conch. Although the islands are difficult to reach and have few hotels, more tourists arrive every year. The islanders hope to find a way to increase their income from tourism without surrendering their colony's remote, undeveloped charm.

Claimed for Spain by Juan Ponce de León in 1512, the Turks and Caicos remained undeveloped until 1678, when Bermudian settlers started a salt-panning industry. The islands were part of the Bahamas colony during the early 1800s, a dependency of Jamaica from 1874 to 1959, and again administered by the Bahamas from 1965 to 1973. Today, they are under direct British control. The island government voted in 1980 to become independent, but anti-independence parties won later elections and the idea has been shelved.

Their environment may be rich in natural beauty, but many West Indians—like this farmer in Grenada—feel the pinch of poverty.

Problems and Promises

Jean-Baptiste Labat, a French missionary who served in the French West Indies in the 1700s, said that Grenada "was all that man could desire. To live there was to live in Paradise." In many ways, this is true of all the West Indies. The islands have splendid climates, great natural beauty, and a profusion of delicious foods from land and sea. These qualities have made them a vacation paradise for the rest of the world.

For most West Indians, however, life is not paradise. Farmers must till poor or exhausted soil to produce crops that may be swept away by the next storm. Individual fishermen cannot always compete in the marketplace with large commercial fleets. And many West Indians, with no wish to farm or no land to call their own, cannot find jobs. Some islands are richer than others, but poverty and unemployment are problems throughout the region.

Other problems exist as well: unstable governments in many of the newly independent nations and political unrest in some of the islands that are not yet independent; occasional outbursts of racial tension, caused by the fact that most blacks are poorer than most whites; and the lack of resources, which means that few of the islands

This Jamaican woodcarver and other craftspeople contribute to the island's economy with sales to tourists.

can earn enough income to give their people a comfortable standard of living. Health care, education, and housing need improvement in many West Indian states.

Tourism and technology offer the best hopes for improving the lives of West Indians. If government planners carefully develop their country's tourist industries, the islands can remain lovely yet still offer tropical vacations to people from around the world. Development must strike a balance between the need for hotels, roads, and airports and the need to preserve natural beauty and clear waters. The promise of technology lies in new industries, most notably the manufacturing of microchips for computers and other electronic components. These industries could use imported materials, would require little space, and would produce little pollution. Many of the islands have formed committees to investigate such industries and bring foreign investors to the West Indies.

Many people believe that the West Indies' best hope of solving its problems lies in unity among the islands. As tiny, isolated, individual states they lack power, but as a single Caribbean nation they could pool their talents and resources to help each other economically and politically. Six British colonies once attempted to form a common state by organizing the Federation of the West Indies. It failed because Jamaica and Trinidad, the two largest islands, with the most resources, did not believe that they should have to support their smaller and weaker neighbors. Because so many West Indian nations are struggling with troubled economies and social problems, they appear to have little interest in looking outside their own borders toward a unified Caribbean.

Nevertheless, the Caribbean region is unified culturally, if not politically. Its many ethnic groups, languages, religions, and cultures have merged into a common Creole bond that, to some degree, links all West Indians. The West Indies have been a giant experiment in human chemistry, in which many ingredients have been mixed to-

Grenadian steel-band music is just one of the unique art forms of Creole culture, in which people and traditions from many lands have met and merged.

gether to form a new element. In spite of the conflicts between nations and races that have marred Caribbean history, the experiment continues.

Many sociologists (scientists who study the ways people interact in societies) believe that the West Indies are a model of what world society may evolve toward in the 21st century. They point to the increased migration of individuals and large groups from one country to another, the increase in marriages between people of different nationalities or races, and the rising use of electronic communications (such as television, telephones, and e-mail) to link all parts of the world together. These factors, they say, may one day create a "global Creole" culture made up of elements from hundreds of different peoples and ways of life. If so, the West Indies will have led the way.

‹ G L O S S A R Y ›

archipelago	An island chain.
caiman	A crocodile native to the Caribbean region, now extinct in many areas. The Cayman Islands take their name from this reptile.
calypso	A form of Creole music that is lively and fast-moving, with a syncopated beat. Calypso has become a popular dance music in many parts of the world.
cay	Pronounced "key." An islet, or small island, that is usually part of a larger island group.
Commonwealth of Nations	Formerly the British Commonwealth, this international organization consists of the United Kingdom and many of its former colonies and dependencies. Commonwealth nations share favorable trade regulations and defense treaties. The British monarch is still the formal head of state of many independent Commonwealth nations, but exercises no real power of government.
Creole	From the Spanish *criollo*, meaning "locally raised." The term was once used to refer to colonists who had been born in the colonies, as opposed to those who had emigrated from the parent country. Today, it refers to the culture and languages of the West Indies, which have borrowed elements from European, African, and Asian countries.

jibaros   Peasant farmers of the Puerto Rican interior.

latifundios   Large estates worked by slave or peasant labor in the Spanish colonies.

leeward   The side of an island that is sheltered from the prevailing winds. In the West Indies, the southern and western coasts are leeward.

Maroon   A term used for a runaway slave in the early colonies. Runaway slaves formed communities in the remote, hilly regions of Jamaica and Haiti, often intermarrying with the local Indians. The largest surviving Maroon community today is in Jamaica.

mestizo   The Spanish word for a person of mixed race.

Papiamento   The patois of the Netherlands Antilles. It is based on Spanish and contains elements of Dutch, Portuguese, French, and African languages.

patois   A local language based on two or more other languages. Many West Indians speak English or another official language at work or school but a Creole patois, perhaps based on French and West African, at home.

reggae   Jamaican music with a distinctive, syncopated beat. The lyrics often deal with religion and social injustice. Reggae became internationally popular in the 1970s and has influenced musicians around the world.

solfaratas   Volcanic vents, or fissures, in the ground from which steam and gases escape. Dominica has many solfaratas.

tenantries   Communities for agricultural workers on Barbados. The workers own their houses but rent the plots of land on which the houses are built.

The tenantries usually border large farming estates.

Voudoun, or Voodoo A religion practiced throughout the West Indies but most widespread in Haiti, where it has had much political and social power. Voudoun combines some Christian elements with African beliefs in spirits and sorcery.

zemis Small stone statues that represent the gods and spirits of the Arawak Indians.

‹INDEX›

PICTURE CREDITS